Free Rum On The Congo: And What It Is Doing There

William Temple Hornaday

FREE RUM

ON THE ©ONGO,

—AND—

WHAT IT IS DOING THERE.

By WM. T. HORNADAY,

Author of "Two Years in the Jungle."

"What is being done out there in the name of commerce is a world-crime of a character so colossal, of an immorality so shameless and profound, that if it could be regarded as a type and illustration of nineteenth century civilization it would be necessary to denounce that civilization as a horrible sham, and a conspicuous failure."—*New York Tribune Editorial.*

CHICAGO.
Woman's Temperance Publication Association.
1887.

Introductory Letter.

I have been asked to write an introduction to this book. I know no better introduction than the following appeal made not long ago to Bishop Crowther by one of the most powerful Emirs in the West of Africa through the Rev. C. Paul, a missionary there:

"Salute Crowther, the great Christian minister. After salutation, please tell him he is a father to us in this land; anything he sees will injure us in all this land, he would not like it. This we know perfectly well. The matter about which I am speaking with my mouth, write it; it is as if it is done by my hand. It is not a long matter; it is about barasá (rum or gin). Barasá, barasá, barasá; by God! it has ruined our country; it has ruined our people very much; it has made our people become mad. I have given a law that no one dares buy or sell it; and any one who is found selling it his house is to be eaten up (plundered); any one found drunk will be killed. I have told all the Christian traders that I agree to everything for trade except barasá. I have told Mr. McIntosh's people to say the barasá remaining with them must be returned down the river. Tell Crowther, the great Christian minister, that he is our father. I beg you, Malam Kipo (Mr. Paul), don't forget this writing, because we all beg that he (Crowther) should beg the great priests (Committee C. M. S.) that they should beg the English Queen to prevent bringing barasá into this land.

"For God and the Prophet's sake! for God and the Prophet His messenger's sake, he must help us in this matter—that of barasá. We have all confidence in him. He must not leave our country· to become spoiled by barasá. Tell him, may God bless him in his work. This is the mouth-word from Maliké, the Emir of Nupé."

No stronger appeal than this could possibly be made to Christian hearts! If we profess to be followers of that Saviour who was "not willing that any should perish," with what an enthusiasm of love and pity should we throw ourselves into the breach for the defense of these, our poor defenseless brethren, against the onslaught of this terrible curse!

Canon Farrar, in a recent article in the *Contemporary Review* (July, 1887,) compares the old curse of the slave trade to the present curse of the liquor traffic, and declares the latter to be far more deadly. He says, "The old rapacity of the slave trade has been followed by the greedier and more ruinous rapacity of the drink-seller. Our fathers tore from the neck of Africa a yoke of whips; we have subjected the native races to a yoke of scorpions. * * * We have opened the rivers of Africa to commerce, only to pour down them that 'raging Phlegethon of alcohol,' than which no river of the Inferno is more blood-red or more accursed. * * * Is the conscience of the nation dead? If not, will no voice be raised of sufficient power to awaken it from a heavy sleep?"

Canon Farrar has thus raised his voice in England. This little book of Mr. Hornaday's is the raising of a voice in America which I earnestly pray may awaken the conscience of our people and our Government, and compel them to enlist with one accord in a crusade against this diabolical traffic, which, for the sake of gain to a few traders, is ruining the bodies and souls of the helpless races of conquered Africa.

Mr. Hornaday has made a careful study of the whole subject, and is therefore well qualified to speak. He told me, when we first conversed on the subject, that his soul had been so stirred within him by the dreadful facts he had discovered, that he had determined to fight for his African brethren single-handed and alone, if necessary, until their deliverance was accomplished.

Surely the Christians of America will be ready to join him, when once this book has had an opportunity to tell its heart-rending story.

A Petition is being sent out by the World's Woman's Christian Temperance Union, and all Societies of every kind are urged to have it signed by their officers, and forwarded to me at 1305 Arch Street, Philadelphia, Pa.

HANNAH WHITALL SMITH,

Am. Sec. World's W. C. T. U.

Contents.

CHAPTER V.

CHAPTER VI.

CHAPTER VII.

CHAPTER VIII.

Introduction.

This little book was not written to beguile an idle hour, nor to furnish either entertainment or amusement. In the charitable supposition that the facts it sets forth are known to but few, and felt by still fewer, its purpose is to inform humane men and women of the gigantic evil that is being perpetrated in the jungles of equatorial Africa. It is confidently believed by the author that when once public attention is attracted to the devil's work being done on the Congo in the name of commerce and civilization, there will arise a host of champions to enter the lists on the side of humanity. It cannot be possible that the Christian nations of the nineteenth century, which have washed from their robes all stains of slavery and serfdom, will calmly countenance the deliberate, systematic debauchment of fifty millions of ignorant savages by the agencies of our sadly imperfect civilization. It cannot be that men's consciences have become so seared, their hearts so hardened, and their milk of human kindness so dried up.

We have seen many great wrongs inflicted upon helpless people in the name of commerce, but none excepting slavery equal to the flooding of Africa with a tidal wave of cheap and deadly rum.

It is amazing that the representatives of any enlightened nation could insist upon regulations allowing the exportation of poisonous brandy to Africa in an unlimited quantity, and free of all duty. The result of the Berlin West

African Conference, when stripped of all diplomatic drapery, was simply this; the trading nations gave themselves a free entry into the country, by their accursed free trade enactments they utterly pauperized the government of the Congo Free State (as a reward for the efforts of the International African Association in opening up the country!), and they fastened the free rum traffic upon the people for twenty years. Let him deny these facts who can. The African trader is not half so much to blame for the commercial crime being committed in Africa as are the manufacturers and shippers of the liquor, and the statesmen and friends of man who allow the infernal business to go on.

The evil here complained of can be remedied. Every one who reads these pages can do something toward the accomplishment of that end. It is not enough to feel indignant and sympathetic, and merely say, " Be ye warmed and fed." Deeds are required as well as words. Responsibilities cannot be shifted or shirked without incurring personally a share of the disgrace which will fall upon the Christian world in general if this devil's work is not suppressed. It remains to be seen, therefore, whether our boasted civilization is, morally, an earnest, honest reality, or a hypocritical sham.

I take pleasure in acknowledging here my indebtedness to the courtesy of our Department of State in procuring for me from various officers in our foreign diplomatic service much valuable information, which I would otherwise have found it extremely difficult to obtain. My thanks are also due the New York *Tribune* for permission to quote in these chapters various portions of my letter on " Free Rum on the Congo," which appeared in the issue of that journal for July 18, 1886.   W. T. H.

Le Droit Park, Washington, D. C., March 15, 1887.

CHAPTER I.

The Effect of Civilization on Savage Tribes.

We have before us the consideration of a grave and even mournful subject. It is no less than a trial for impeachment of our self-righteous civilization, in so far as it affects the savage tribes of Africa. Facts are stubborn, and often disagreeable; but if we have true manhood we must meet them face to face. Let cowards shirk the encounter and sophists befog it, after the manner of the cuttle-fish, with an inpenetrable cloud of theories, if they must; but the dragon that threatens to devour the people of Africa shall be unmasked and revealed in all his hideousness.

The idea that civilization is an unmitigated blessing to be sought after by every savage, is one of the dearest delusions of this age. It comes to us in early childhood, grows with our growth, and never leaves us until we part with life. We are taught that if a savage cannot achieve civilization, it must be thrust upon him. He must be taught to wear

clothes, to read, and do as we do in as many re-
spects as possible. As soon as he is clothed, he is
admittedly in his right mind also, and his future is
assured.

This fondly cherished fallacy has wrought incalculable damage to many savage tribes that were
worthy of being let alone. When will men ever
learn that it is better to let a race of people live on
and thrive in the blissful ignorance of savagery
than to civilize it off the face of the earth? To
very many primitive tribes, civilization has proved
a curse of the first magnitude. Had I omnipotent
power, and a wish to wreak vengeance on the natives of Africa, no seven vials of wrath could be
poured out upon them which would be more deadly than our own boasted unchristian civilization.
Were I a king of naked savages on the Congo or
the Zambesi, I would resist the Caucasian to the
death. No white man except a missionary should
ever enter my territory and live. It would be far
better for me and my people to die of bullets than
brandy.

Reader, do you sneer at the above, or throw
down this book in unspeakable disgust? If your
mind is open to conviction, pray let us go on together, while I give my reasons. They will constitute a picture of the effects of civilization on
savage tribes.

The trouble is simply this: nearly all the savage tribes accept the virtues of civilization at retail and the vices at wholesale. Too much attention is paid to their education for good, and not enough to their *protection from evil*. Just as an ignorant emigrant learns first the oaths and obscenity of the new language he encounters, so does the savage first learn drunkenness and new forms of debauchery from the civilization which touches him, long before he has an opportunity to learn anything else. In ninety-nine cases out of a hundred, his first news of the Christian world is brought by a trader, who also brings him fire-water and gunpowder. As to the moral character of the trader, that shall form the subject of a separate chapter.

Our civilization, as it stands at present, is a wholesale exterminator of savage races. They are killed off by intemperance, and modern diseases of various kinds, which are introduced among them by unprincipled Europeans, aided by other causes, less reprehensible but no less deadly, which spring from the same source. The sole object of this effort, therefore, is to show that it is the sacred duty of the better part of civilized mankind to protect the people of Africa from total destruction, body and soul, at the hands of the worse than heathen liquor shippers and traders.

But let us take a case by way of illustration. This is what Dr. Emil Holub has to say of certain savage tribes he encountered in South Africa:

"Within the last ten years, and especially since the introduction of spirituous liquors into the country, wherever the Hottentot element has mingled with the Bantu, or whenever the Batlapins, Barolongs, or other kindred tribes have not had capable and responsible men for their chiefs, they have been corrupted by the Korannas, Griquas, and others, *who have adopted all the vices and uone of the virtues of the white men.* The consequence has been that drunkenness, idleness, robbery, and even murder, HAVE BECOME rife among them." (*Seven Years in South Africa. I., p. 250.*)

"As we wended our way down the slope, we came within view of another native village [of Batlapins]. The mere sight of our wagon served to put its population into a state of extreme excitement. A whole crowd of men in tattered European clothes, except now and then one in a mangy skin, followed by as many women, all naked except for little leather aprons, and by a swarm of children as naked as when they were born, came shouting eagerly toward us. They were nearly all provided with bottles, or pots or cans, and cried out for brandy. 'Suppy, suppy, bas, verkup Brandwen!' they repeated impatiently.

" They had brought all manner of things to barter for spirits. One man held up a jackal's hide, another a goat skin; another offered us bullock's thongs; yet another had a bullock yoke; and some of them had their home-made wooden spoons and platters to dispose of to us. It was a disgusting scene. We tried to treat the whole matter with contempt, and to take no notice of their demand; but when we attempted to drive on, their importunities waxed louder than ever. They caught hold of the bridles, and pushed the oxen back, becoming ever more and more clamorous. One of the men made what he evidently imagined would be an irresistible appeal by offering me a couple of greasy shillings. They next tried to bribe us with some skins of milk, which the women were made to bring out from the huts, and they were driven to despair when they found that the offer of a goat that they dragged forward was not accepted.

" Their screechings and shoutings were of no avail; not a drop of fire-water was to be extorted from me. We had almost to beat them off before they would allow us to proceed. A few persevered in following us to the ford, and made a final effort to secure one bottle by a private negotiation, out of sight of their neighbors. They con-

fidentially offered five shillings for the bottle, but
I was inexorable. (*Ibid. p. 235.*)

"Lazy and dirty, crafty and generally untruth-
ful, living without a thought beyond the immediate present, capable of well-nigh any crime for
the sake of fire-water—to my mind they [the Ko-
rannas] offer an example of humanity as degraded
and loathsome as can be imagined. Employ them
in the far wilderness, *where no European is at
hand to supply them with spirits,* and it is possible that they might be found more desirable than
Kaffres for cattle-drivers or horse-breakers; but after making several trials of them myself, and using every effort to keep them sober, I was always
compelled to give up in despair.

"It is only when he is utterly without the means
of procuring the brandy, which is his sole and engrossing desire, that a Koranna is ever known to
rouse himself from his habitual sloth. * * * *As
a distinct race, the Korannas are dying out.* In
this respect they are sharing the lot of the Hottentots proper, who dwell in Cape Colony and
Griqualand. So continual has been the dimunition
of their number, that they are not half what they
formerly were, and their possessions have diminished in a still greater proportion." (*Ibid. p. 98.*)

The following will serve to show what commerce and civilization have already accomplished amongst the coast negroes of West Africa:

" A people so thoroughly debased, demoralized, degraded," as the natives of the delta of the Niger, "I could not have conceived existed within a few miles of parts which British ships have frequented for a century. But it only adds another to former proofs that the intercourse between civilized and savage nations has hitherto been productive of anything but good to the latter. (*Laird and Oldfield*, *I.*, *p. 107.*)

" I was much struck by the extreme demoralization and barbarism of the inhabitants [of Calabar] in comparison with the natives of the interior. The human skulls that are seen in every direction, and that are actually kicking about the streets, attest the depravity of feeling among the people, and add another to the long list of melancholy proofs of the debasing effects of European intercourse." (*Ibid. I., p. 277.*)

The following are a few summarized observations drawn from the testimony of many travelers by Mr. Herbert Spencer, as they are recorded in his " Descriptive Sociology":

The Kaffres.—" The farther removed the natives are from European influence, the higher they are. Craft, faithlessness and begging are not national traits, but the result of intercourse with whites. In commercial transactions, honorable and trustworthy wherever they have not been deceived by whites."

The Inland Negroes.—" Except where they have had much intercourse with whites, the negroes cannot be accused of being specially addicted to intoxicating liquors!" (*Waitz II., p. 86.*) "The Foolahs and Mandingos very strictly abstain from fermented liquors, which they hold in such abhorrence that if a single drop were to fall upon a clean garment it would be rendered unfit to wear until washed." (*Winterbottom I., p. 72.*)

Fortunately for our purpose, we have before us the statistics of several isolated communities of people which show us in plain figures the degree of rapidity with which the vices and customs of civilization are capable of exterminating some savage tribes. I dedicate them especially to the optimists who believe that civilization is to the savage the embodiment of all blessings both in this world and the next. The facts given below are from Mr. A. R. Wallace's "Australasia," and relate to people of certain islands in the Pacific Ocean who have had civilization thrust upon them.

"*The Marquesas Islanders* appear to have suffered severely from their contact with European vices, customs and civilization, their numbers in

1850 having been estimated at 50,000, while, according to a recent geographical work, they are now [1880] reduced to less than 4,000." (*p. 523.*)

" *Tahiti.*—One chief cause, probably, of the decreasing numbers of these people is the prevalence of habits of intoxication, in which they indulge as a substitute for the dance and song, and various amusements so injudiciously forbidden by the missionaries. A recent French traveler, M. Jules Garnier, informs us that the Tahitians now seek the mere sensual pleasure of intoxication, unenlivened by the social enjoyments of their ancient festivals. *Most fatal gift of all, they have been taught to ferment the juice of the orange*, and thus produce a liquor with which to obtain the pleasures and penalties of intoxication, which men, women and children alike enjoy and suffer. The orange has been for these people as the forbidden fruit of the Garden of Eden—the tree of good and evil." (*p. 511.*)

The Marshall Islands.—" The people resemble those of the Caroline Islands, but have been as yet less demoralized by contact with foreign vice and disease." (*p. 535.*)

New Zealand, The Maoris. —" They cannot as a body compete with Europeans. Our habits are not suited to them; our diseases and vices decimate them; their numbers diminish year by year,

and, as in many other cases, we seem to civilize and
Christianize only to destroy. When first taken
possession of in 1840, New Zealand is supposed to
have contained near 100,000 Maoris. In 1856
there were but 65,000; in 1874 they had decreased
to 45,740, and it is believed that they are now
diminishing still more rapidly. Should, however,
the present rate of decrease continue, it will not
take more than 150 years to bring about the total
extinction of this interesting race." (*p. 569.*)

The Society Islands.—" When first visited by
Europeans, they [the people] appear to have been
remarkably healthy, and the islands were very
populous. Captain Cook estimated that the Society Islands then possessed 1,700 war-canoes,
manned by 68,000 men. Now the total population
of the group is said to be only 9,000! Such has
been the effect of contact with European civilization on a people declared by our great navigator,
Cook, to have been ' liberal, brave, open and can-
did, without either suspicion or treachery, cruelty
or revenge;' while the naturalist, Forster, who accompanied him, declared that he ' never saw any of
a morose or discontented disposition in the whole
nation;' and that 'they all join to their cheerful
temper, a politeness and elegance which is happily
blended with the most innocent simplicity of manners.' How sad it is that a people with so many

admirable qualities should be exterminated before our eyes by the relentless march of our too imperfect civilization."—(*p. 496.*)

The Friendly Islands.—" The people are now all Christians, but, as in almost every other instance, they are diminishing in numbers. In 1847, the population was estimated by the missionaries at 40,000 or 50,000, which has now diminished to about 10,000." (*p. 500.*)

Lest some one should hastily and ill-advisedly draw the conclusion that *true Christianity* or the methods of the missionaries are in any way to blame for this wholesale extermination, I hasten to quote another paragraph, which brings us to the root of the whole matter. I submit it as being the most pertinent of all.

The Savage Islanders.—"They are now wholly converted to Christianity, and are found to be a very intelligent, mild and interesting race, and by no means the dangerous savages they were long supposed to be. Their numbers in 1864 were over 5,000, and they are said to increase at the rate of two and a half per cent. annually. If this be true, we may probably attribute it to the fact that the island is too small to attract visitors other than missionaries; and it becomes most valuable evidence that Polynesians may be civilized without being exterminated, if they are only protected from the rude competition, the vices and the diseases which free intercourse with the ordinary class of Europeans invariably brings upon them." (*Australasia. p. 505.*)

I could cite numerous other tribes as examples of the manner in which savages are civilized off the face of the earth; but surely it is unnecessary. Those who care to pursue this question further will do well to study the Tasmanians, the Sandwich Islanders, the Hervey Islanders, the Hottentots, the Aborigines of Australia, and various tribes of Eskimo, Indians and Africans, which there is not even space to name here. If any one doubts the truth, or attempts to weaken the force of the assertion that the vices and diseases of our boasted civilization blights savages like a curse, and sweeps them out of existence by wholesale, the evidence can be piled mountains high.

What was the Christian world's first gift to the African savage? Slavery. One hundred years from now, posterity will look back with horror upon the period of African slavery, and be lost in amazement while trying to divine how intelligent human beings could be so heartless and cruel. When they read the sickening horrors of the slave trade, how over 100,000 men, women and children were stolen every year from their native jungles, branded like cattle, crowded between the decks of slave-ships, far worse than swine in stock-cars to-day, dying by hundreds on every ship by foul air, hunger and thirst, and flung overboard like so many dead dogs,—when they read of this, I say, they will stand aghast and cry, "Why did not the Christian world rise up as one man to stop this fiendish traffic? Where was the curse of God?"

I leave entirely out of consideration the question of slavery on the plantation. The, civilized nations of the world have grappled with that evil and purged themselves of it forever. The most have paid the penalty in money. We, who were so indifferent to the sin in general and to the slave trade horror in particular, *just as we are now to the rum traffic on the Congo,*—we alas! have paid for our high crimes against humanity in blood, and tears, and ashes, as well as treasure.

He who has knowledge of an intended crime, and the power to prevent its execution, becomes an accomplice of the criminal if he allows the crime to be committed. If we fail to suppress the rum traffic in Africa, we are guilty of criminal negligence. At present, it is not a general responsibility; it is individual. It is a matter for *you and me.* It is our duty to do our utmost to awaken public opinion on the subject, and in this way enlist an army of aggressive workers which can move governments to action.

The record of what the white man has done in
Africa is enough to make every Caucasian blush
to own his color, and hang his head in shame.
First the slave trade, now, wholesale intemperance.
The former flourished for nearly three centuries,
and it was not until 1808 that the two most enlightened nations in the world, England and the United
States, decided to suppress the most stupendous
crime that was ever perpetrated against poor humanity. Is this to be set down to their credit? No,
not for one moment. They gave slavery to Africa
in the first place (or at least the Christian world
did), and the taking away of it only squared a very
small proportion of the account. The wrongs it
had inflicted on a helpless people, the lives it had
cost, and the human misery it had entailed, will
never be known in this world, but if they are all
set down in the books of the Most High, it will be
a sad day for even the Christians of those days, to
say nothing of the others, when the judgment is
set, the books are opened, and the accounts balanced.

The mainspring of slavery and the slave trade
was—money. Thank heaven that our share of
that black business is over and done. But no sooner
is the African native protected at one point, than
he is attacked in another. Now his country is being flooded with cheap and deadly rum, gin and
brandy, of which he is passionately fond. He is

snatched from one altar, only to be sacrificed on another, under the hypocritical pretense of " opening up " his country to the march of civilization, and all the blessings that flow from " trade;" he is being supplied abundantly with the means of making a hopeless drunkard of himself, and sinking him lower than he is even now, until he finally disappears from the earth. You may clothe him, educate him, convert him to Christianity; aye, civilize him wholly in every respect if you please, but just so sure as you do not keep liquor away from him, he is a lost man, body and soul. He will go just as the Korannas are going, surely and swiftly. It needs no seer to forecast the future of the Congo native if his supply of civilized (?) liquor is not stopped, and at once. Read the opinion of Count Van der Straten, as given before the great West African Conference at Berlin in 1885.

" The Belgian plenipotentiary said that the indigenous races of the free zone must be sober, or soon cease to exist. There was, moreover, a difference between the effects produced by alcoholism upon the Indian races on the one part and the African races on the other. The negro does not yield physically to drunkenness; he succumbs morally. *If the Powers do not save him from this vice they will make of him a monster who will destroy the work of the Conference.*"

The powers in conference assembled, elected to do nothing whatsoever to "save him from this vice," and the rum-sellers are now hard at work making a monster of him. Just who they are and how they are doing it will be found in other chapters.

CHAPTER II.

THE "OPENING-UP" OF AFRICA, AND THE
PIONEERS OF CIVILIZATION.

The world of commerce is reaching out with
eager hands for the treasures that lie hidden in
the heart of Africa. With marvellous rapidity
the Dark Continent is being explored and "opened-
up." By the recent German annexation of the
country between Cape Frio and Cape Colony,
the coast colonies have been welded together in
one unbroken chain, stretching from the Senegal
around the Cape and up to Abyssinia, or more
than half way around Africa. From every direction, the traders are pressing forward toward the
heart of the wilderness, establishing permanent
lines of communication as they go, to serve as so
many channels by which to drain off the riches of
nature. The basin of the Congo has been chosen
as the scene of a grand assault made by the forces
of an International Association, under the leader-
ship of a king and of Africa's greatest explorer.

The commercial world is opening up Africa
with a vengeance. It is spurred forward on one

side by the prospect of finding a vast market for
the sale of its manufactures at good round prices;
and on the other by the immense stores of natural
products to be purchased of the natives and sold
again at great profit. The manufacturers of Low-
ell and Manchester want to find a market for their
cotton goods; those of Sheffield and Birmingham
for their cutlery, cheap guns and gunpowder, and
the distillers of Hamburg, Amsterdam and New
England want to sell their gin, rum, brandy and
whisky. At the same time they are doubly anxious
to buy palm oil, India rubber, camwood, gum
copal and ivory from the natives, and thus make
a double profit.

It is quite unnecessary to take any special steps
for the commercial development of Africa, for all
the forces of the world combined could not prevent its being opened up right speedily by the irresistible trader. Now that their markets are failing
elsewhere, the effete monarchies of Europe are
turning hopefully to the dusky millions of Central
Africa. So great and so irresistible are the demands
of commerce it is perfectly safe to predict that ere
the close of the next quarter of a century, we will
see a line of steam transit crossing the continent
by rail and river from the mouth of the Congo
on one side to Zanzibar on the other. Nyangwe
and Ujiji will be brought nearer to us than Cal-

cutta, and all the blank spaces in the map of the country will be filled up. There will be stations and European traders everywhere, and also missionaries here and there; but as usual the latter will be too few and far between.

The prospects of the immediate opening up of Africa on a grand scale are so well known as to render it needless to rehearse them. Germany is making an attack on the Zanzibar side; Portugal from the Zambesi coast on the southeast; England from the south, and all Europe from the west. Now let us pause for a moment and see where we stand.

We are on the point of bringing our imperfect civilization in contact with untold millions of ignorant savages. If there are, as estimated by Stanley, 43,000,000 people in the basin of the Congo, it is making a low estimate to say that in twenty years a hundred millions of blacks will have felt the influence of European and American morals and manners. And what shall the harvest be? Ten years from now it will be too late to offer the Africans any protection from the evils that are now being sown amongst them. Shall we do our duty now, while it is possible to accomplish great good, or leave our duty undone until the mischief is accomplished and all is lost, save the few brands that can be plucked from the burning by the missionaries?

In the previous chapter, I tried to show the terrible effect upon savage races of the vices, diseases and bad morals generally of our modern civilization. In order that all may know just what to expect in Africa, unless something is done, I propose to show what kind of men are often found in the advance guard of European commercial pioneers (mind, I do not say wholly composing it), which is already operating in Africa. To save myself from being contradicted, I will quote the words of eye-witnesses only, and in every case stick closely to the text.

Directly south of the Congo Free State, lies an immense territory under the dominion of Portugal. On the other side of the continent, embracing more than half the whole region between Zanzibar and the Cape, and as far south coastwise as Zululand, is another vast area also claimed by Portugal, or 700,000 square miles in all. It is well known that Portuguese traders are more numerous in Africa than those of any other European nationality, and they penetrate farthest into the interior. Do you wish to know what they are, morally? A Portuguese officer, Major Serpa Pinto, on an official exploration through Africa, thus describes them in his book, "How I Crossed Africa," Vol. ii., p. 65.

"Those Portuguese traders who penetrate most deeply into the interior of the African continent, cease, when they do so, to be Portuguese at all. I mean that they are convicts, fellows who have broken out. of prisons on the coast,—men whom society has deprived of the guarantees of citizenship; wretches on whom a sentence of infamy has been passed, and whom justice has branded with the mark of Cain; robbers and assassins whom their country has cast out of her bosom with horror, who should still be carrying the convict's chain allotted to them in their place of bondage, and who on escaping from the territory where the finger of scorn of every civilized man was pointed at them, have fled into these remote regions to seek among savages the refuge they have forfeited, and there to continue a life of crime. Such men cannot be said to dishonor their country, because they have no country to dishonor."

And yet, to the ignorant savage, these men are civilized Christians (!) and as such are looked up to!

So much for the Portuguese side of the question, and let me tell you it is about ten times as broad as people generally suppose. South of the Congo and the Lualaba, the whole country is infested with Portuguese traders, from Benguela to the Zambesi, and from thence to the coast colonies of

Portugal on the southeast. Owing to the fact that these traders most quickly and easily revert back toward the barbarism from which they sprang, they, more than the traders of any other nationality, are able to meet the native on his own ground, and penetrate to remote and dangerous regions that have thus far remained totally inaccessible to English traders, and even to our most daring explorers. The Portuguese go everywhere, seemingly, and trade in everything, including slaves. They have fallen upon southern Africa like a curse. Whenever their vicious habits are adopted, the savage sinks below the level of the brute. Whenever their blood mingles with that of the native, the result is a monster in human form, having all the devilish cunning, cruelty and vice of both races, and the good qualities of neither.

Here is a picture of a sample-specimen, as sketched by Commander V. L. Cameron, in his book " Across Africa."

"With Kasongo [a native king] returned the horde of ruffians who had accompanied him on his plundering raids, and to Lourenzo de Souza Coimbra, a son of Major Coimbra, of Bihé, must be awarded the palm of having reached the highest grade of ruffianism amongst them all.

" He lost no time in coming to see me, in the endeavor to swindle me out of something, and

commenced by advancing a claim to be paid as a
guide, on the plea that he had *shown Alvez* [an-
other trader] the road by which we intended to
reach the coast. * * * * His attire and general appearance were worthy of his character.
A dirty, greasy, and tattered wide-awake hat,
battered shapeless and so far gone that a *chiffon-
nier* would have passed it by as worthless, crowned
this distinguished person. His shirt was equally
dirty, and a piece of grass-cloth bound round his
waist trailed its end upon the ground. His hair
was short and kinky, and his almost beardless face
was of a dirty yellow color. Even had he not
been always in a half-drunken state, his blood-shot
eye would have told the tale of debauchery. In
short, he was true to his appearance, an unmitigated ruffian." * * * "Coimbra returned
soon after, and. I discovered that he knew
nothing concerning the house, but had been engaged on some plundering and murdering expedition in company with a party of Kasongo's
people." * * * "Coimbra, who had been
backwards and forwards with Kasongo, now left
the caravan to plunder, and obtain a batch of
slaves to take to Bihé."

This is an individual portrait. Here is a statement from the same author, who has seen more of

the Portuguese territory than any other Englishman, which covers the whole ground:

"On this march with Alvez [another Portuguese
half-breed] I was disgusted beyond measure with
what I saw of the manner in which the unfortu-
nate slaves were treated [A. D. 1875], and have
no hesitation in asserting that the WORST OF THE
ARABS *are, in this respect, angels of light in
comparison with the Portuguese and those who
travel with them.*"

As a forcible illustration of how the devil's
work is being done in the heart of Africa, and the
account to which it is being charged, I must quote
another page from Commander Cameron's book,
pausing only to remind the reader that the same
deeds are being perpetrated there to-day:

"Coimbra arrived in the afternoon, with a gang
of *fifty-two women*, tied together in lots of seventeen or eighteen.

"Some had children in arms, others were far
advanced in pregnancy, and all were laden with
huge bundles of grass-cloth and other plunder.
These poor weary and foot-sore creatures were
covered with weals and scars, showing how un-
mercifully cruel had been the treatment received at
the hands of the savage who called himself their
owner.

" The misery and loss of life entailed by the
capture of these women is far greater than can be
imagined, except by those who have witnessed
such heart-rending scenes. Indeed, the cruelties
perpetrated in the heart of Africa by men calling
themselves Christians, and carrying the Portuguese
flag, can scarcely be credited by those living in a
civilized land; and the government of Portugal
cannot be cognizant of the atrocities committed by
men claiming to be her subjects.

"To obtain these fifty-two women, at least ten
villages had been destroyed, each having a population of from one to two hundred, or about fifteen
hundred in all. Some may, perchance, have es-
caped to neighboring villages; but the greater
portion were undoubtedly burnt when their villages were surprised, shot while attempting to
save their wives and families, or doomed to die of
starvation in the jungle, unless some wild beast
put a more speedy end to their miseries."

Here is what Cameron writes of another pioneer
of civilization, Joao Baptista Ferreira, a Portuguese of Bihé, and a very important personage in
that country:

"Indeed, I must acknowledge that to me and
mine he showed great kindness, and I wish I were
not compelled, in the interest of Africa, to make
any allusions to the dark side of his character.

But *fais ce que dois advienne que pourra.* I am constrained to declare that he was anything but the right kind of a man to create a good impression by trading in Africa. *Hé was openly engaged in the slave traffic, notwithstanding his holding a commission from the Portuguese government as a district judge; and slaves in chains were to be seen in his settlement.*"

"With my experience of the manner in which slaves are obtained, I could not but feel pained that white men, who could thus disregard the feelings of fellow-creatures, should be amongst the *first specimens of Europeans seen by the untutored people of the interior.*"

In the presence of the horrors of the slave trade, the sale of liquors to the natives sinks, for the moment, into comparative insignificance. But, after all, it bids fair to become the deadlier evil of the two; for while the Coimbras kill by the hundred, fire-water slays by the thousand, souls and bodies together. It is better for a savage to die at once, by bullet or spear, than to live out a life of drunkenness, debauchery and crime, begetting drunkards and criminals to survive him, and descend to even lower depths than he.

It seems almost like mockery to speak of the liquor traffic in territories where the slave trade still flourishes; but the two evils are twins, and should be strangled together. In the record of his journey from Bihé to Benguela, on the coast, Cameron mentions aguardienté and the drunkenness of the natives no less than twelve times. In one place it was a meeting with a caravan coming up with "a large stock of aguardienté;" at another it was his total inability to purchase food for himself and his people, because the natives "wanted only powder and aguardienté in exchange," and he had neither to give; anon it is a meeting with a drunken king, or with parties of Bihé traders who were "drunk and abusive," and who, in some instances, "attempted to rob my stragglers." It seemed that almost the sole article of commerce desired from the coast was aguardienté. Witness the following:

"On this march we met no less than ten up-caravans, numbering seventy to eighty men each (*i. e.*, 700 to 800 men). They were principally laden with small bags of salt, and bottles and kegs of aguardienté, which they had purchased at Benguela." * * * "At this camp we were joined by many Bailunda, bound for Benguela, with flour to exchange for aguardienté."

But enough of the Portuguese territory at present. Let us see what kind of examples were set by the English and American pioneers of civilization, a few years ago. Here is a page from Monteiro's "Angola and the River Congo," (p. 298).*

"The English and other foreigners on the coast make use of too much brandy and spirits, which is the principal cause of the sickness amongst them; but I am happy to say that drunkenness has very greatly decreased of late years. It would not be easy to see, now, such scenes as I·have witnessed at Quissembo and Kabenda, only a few years ago."

"I was at the former place when an Englishman died from the effects of intemperance, a few hours after his arrival from Kabenda, where a three days' orgie had been held to bid him good-by, previous to his return to England. His body was laid on a table, candles were lit all around it, and a kind of wake ·held nearly all night, during which time two casks of bottled ale and several cases of spirits were consumed, amongst not more

---

*In justice to the European traders of to-day, on the West Coast, it must be impressed upon the reader that the disgusting pictures here quoted from Mr. Monteiro (himself a commercial pioneer) represent a state of semi-barbarism which has passed away. The European traders of to-day are a very different set of men from the debauchees Mr. Monteiro describes. Sharp competition has brought good men to the front, and drunkenness and incompetency are at a discount. Personally, the traders are gentlemen of education, refinement, and ability, and, so far as can be learned, there is nothing to be said against their character,

than a dozen people.   In the morning a hole was
dug in the sand, and the body, in a wooden coffin,
lowered into it, whilst the few English in the place
stood around, most of them crying, and held by
their black servants from falling into the grave,
the effects of the "wake" not allowing them to be
sufficiently steady to stand without assistance.   An
American, since dead, poor fellow, tried to read
the burial service, but he was obliged to give up
the task, his utterance being most amusingly choked
with sobs and hiccoughs."

"I have known an Englishman to invite the
· rest of his countrymen to dinner, on Christmas
day, and only a very small number make their
appearance, the rest having been overpowered
by drink at breakfast and during the day."

"At Kabenda, upon one occasion, a poor fellow
who was dying was taken out of his bed, seated in
a chair at the head of the table, and his head held
up to make him drink to his own health, whilst

---

any more than of the same number of merchants in this
country. As might be expected, they and the missionaries
have little in common, and seem to be natural enemies.
But the traders are not most to blame for the liquor traffic.
It belongs on higher shoulders,—those of the great merchants at home who supply the liquor, and the statesmen
who truckle to them so far as to allow them to do it. The
trader is only the agent of the real offender, and his legislative accomplice.

the rest sang, 'For he is a jolly good fellow.'
Next morning he was found dead and stiff in his
bed."

It is amazing that any man who had witnessed
such things as the above, could have found it in
his heart to write elsewhere, "And let not rum
or gin be abused for its great share in the development of produce, for it is *a powerful incentive to
work*."

Stanley calls strong drink "the bane of Western
Africa," and asserts that the whole western coast
is too much indebted to the ruin effected by intemperance.

In spite of the fact that all his European assist-
tants were selected with the greatest care, according
to the highest standard of requirement in men sent
forth to savage Africa as models of civilization, it
is saddening to read between the lines of "The
Congo" [Vol. II., p. 253] of men who "scented
after impurities," wallowed in mud, proved in-
competent and intemperate, "or were of depraved
nature." "It is well, however, for many of them,"
says the author, "that the expedition did not belong
to some national government, otherwise extreme
measures would often have been taken to curb the
excessive licentiousness to which some were too
prone, and punish severely the many sins of omission and commission of which some were guilty."

It is a sad thought that such things could be true of any out of the mere handful of Europeans who were so carefully selected for the high task of opening up the valley of the Congo, and showing the savages the best side of civilization. It is, indeed, a difficult task to find men who are morally fit to be trusted with the education of a savage. And what must a savage think of a civilization whose pioneers are .guilty of slave-stealing and murder, intemperance, unchastity and general licentiousness, in addition to the still higher crime of sowing all their vices, methods of crime and diseases amongst ignorant people!

Africa is being opened up from all sides, but to what? To Portuguese slave-traders for one thing, and also to New England rum, Holland gin, poisonous brandy from Hamburg, Portuguese aguardienté, and deadly alcohol from France, and God only knows where else. It is also opening up the interior to fire-arms and gunpowder, by means of which the slave-trading few are able to rob, murder and enslave the many to their own hearts' content. Stanley tells in the account referred to in a previous page, how a company of three hundred traders and slaves, all armed with guns, devastated one hundred and eighteen villages and forty-three districts in securing two thousand three hundred slaves (women and children).

He estimates that two thousand five hundred
people were shot, and that at least thirteen hundred
additional deaths were caused in various ways by
the great slaughter.

But for the *fire-arms*, which gave the few mastery
over the many, such frightful carnage and wholesale enslavement could never have been accomplished.

In the previous chapter, I pointed out the effect
of civilization upon the Korannas in South Africa,
and, as a fit ending to this chapter, I will cite
another case from Dr. Holub's "Seven Years in
South Africa." It will serve well to point my
moral, even though it falls far short of adorning a
tale. It is the most virulent case of trader I ever
heard of, and likewise the most aggravating.

Khame, the King of the Bamangwatos, had
passed a law that no liquor should be sold in his
territory under heavy penalty, and also that no trader
having liquor in his possession for sale, should
enter his domain, nor even be permitted to pass
through any portion of it. Just at the time of Dr.
Holub's visit, along came an English trader, Mr.
"X," who smuggled several cases of alcohol into
the territory—"atrocious stuff" which "completely
overpowered Westbeech." Being detected, "X"
was ordered out of the country. After trekking
a short distance, he buried his alcohol, returned,

"lied atrociously" to the king about it, and afterward sold it to the king's subjects. Finally his perfidy was discovered, and he fled; but the king's soldiers hunted him down and captured him. At Shoshong, the capital, Dr. Holub saw the excellent "X" fined £100 for breaking the law, and formally expelled from the territory as dangerous to the community. "At the same sitting, the king fined two trader's agents £10 apiece for being drunk outside their quarters in the outskirts of the town, telling them that if they were determined to drink, they must confine themselves to their own wagons; he, for his part, was quite resolved that they should not make an exhibition of themselves before his subjects."

What a pitiful and heart-saddening spectacle is this of an ignorant African savage struggling with intelligent European Christians (!) to save his people from the horrors of intemperance, a vice thrust upon him by civilization.

In my "Two Years in the Jungle," I took occasion to observe that savage tribes deteriorate morally, physically and numerically according to the degree in which they are influenced by civilization. Well, a good deal to my surprise, this simple statement of a well-known fact excited amongst a few of my reviewers both scoffs and snarls. Indeed, no less a journal than the London

Daily News was led to pronounce these views "somewhat crude," and the author of them "not a social philosopher." And, further, "it is to be hoped that his free-and-easy application of the convenient doctrine of 'the survival of the fittest' will not lead his readers to forget it is the triumph of civilization to protect the weak against the strong."

I quote the above, not from any feeling in the matter, for I have none, but because it fairly voices a mighty popular feeling,—or rather a fallacy, a theory or hallucination, whichever you choose to call it. Come now, let us reason together, with all our prejudices, our pet theories, and our bigotry laid aside. Tell us, my worthy reviewer, how much has civilization protected the weak against the strong drink of the trader, the world over? What it has done on the Congo shall transpire in another chapter.

·What has it done to protect the weak in South Africa, among Khame's people, and the Korannas, for instance? The Cape Calony and Natal people are not slow in legislating for the benefit of trade, but have they ever passed stringent laws against the importation of "atrocious stuff," or prohibited its manufacture or its sale among the natives?

For fear you have not at call an answer to this

question, I beg to offer you one that covers the
whole ground, clipped from the New York
Tribune (Aug. 29). It fits the question as a
black cap fits the face of a murderer.

"The Parliament of Cape Town, Africa, is a
queer body. Not long ago a bill was introduced,
placing restrictions on the sale of brandy, or "cape
smoke," to the natives. But the farmers strongly
objected. 'If,' said they, 'the natives are to be
treated as children, they are not fit to receive the
franchise; if, on the other hand, they are really
men, let them drink all the brandy they want.'
As soon as the restrictive bill was defeated by this
argument, a bill was introduced giving the natives
the franchise; it was at once opposed and defeated
by the same members on the ground that the natives had become drunken sots and were not fit to be
citizens. It may be added that the brandy is supplied to the natives by these high-minded legisla-
tors, most of whom are in the business of making
it, and all of whom are very noisy in their professions of Christianity."

Shame on such Christianity! and shame on
such legislation! If Equatorial Africa is to be
"developed" in the same way as South Africa,
then I say, away with such development! If the
savage cannot be benefited, in God's name *let him
alone*, and let him work out his own salvation

until the time comes when he can be helped without being destroyed.

It is the part of wisdom, of humanity, of true
Christianity to take stringent measures for the protection of aborigines against all such wretches as
the above. Colonies and home governments are
instant, in season and out of season, in protecting
the civil, religious and commercial rights of their
subjects, but where is the one that sets up insur-
mountable barriers of law and order for the protection of the morals of their aborigines? They
protect their lives in one way, it is true, but they
fail to prevent moral murder among them.
What policy can be more short-sighted than that
of the average missionary who goes to work to
translate the Bible and teach theology to a lot of
naked savages while the traders are circulating
vile rum amongst them so freely it is almost an
impossibility to assemble a sober congregation?
It is useless for the teachers to feebly strike the
highest notes on the key-board so long as the
traders are thundering on all the bass keys at the
opposite end.

The African savage must be protected from the
evil influences of unscrupulous traders, or he is
lost. Prompt measures should be taken for the
total suppression of the traffic in spirituous liquors,
of the slave trade, and of the sale of fire-arms and

gunpowder to slave traders or their agents. If this great Christian world, with all its education, wealth and power, cannot find ways and means to accomplish that much, then let all boastings of national greatness, and intelligence, and philantrophy cease forever! If the church alone cannot do that much, then its power is of the earth, and the hand of God is not with it.

CHAPTER III.

THE FOUNDING OF THE CONGO FREE STATE.

In order that we may know every detail of the great task that lies before us and view the field to be fought over, we must scan the records of certain movements affecting Africa.

This, then, is the history, in brief, of the founding of the Congo Free State.

To His Majesty Leopold II., King of the Belgians, belongs the high honor of inaugurating the great movement which resulted, first, in the African International Association and its national committees, then in the Committee of Study of the Upper Congo, which presently became known as the International Association of the Congo, and finally in the Congo Free State itself. He was not only president of both those bodies, but also their chief financial supporter. When has the world witnessed, in recent years, the devotion of a king to a more kingly task, with truer philanthropy, with so utter a lack of self-interest, with such royal liberality? The accumulation of Krupp guns and repeating rifles, palaces and jewels become ignoble pastimes in comparison with a gigantic effort to develop and civilize in reality as well as in name, a vast territory containing forty-three millions of people. Such an enterprise is, indeed, enough to make a reign illustrious. It is enough to make an American believe in kings forever. Long live the King! And it is to him we turn in our quest for a hand powerful enough to strangle the liquor traffic in the Congo Free State.

In September, 1876, while Stanley was crossing Lake Tanganyika on his way across Africa, the King of the Belgians convened, at his palace in Brussels, a conference of distinguished African travelers to devise ways and means by which Equatorial Africa might be explored and opened up to commerce and civilization, and the suppression of the slave trade effected. All agreed that it was necessary to establish and maintain a chain of " hospitable and scientific" stations across Africa, which should serve as a great base line for future explorations and operations in the interior of the continent. Since such a great object would be of vast international benefit when effected, it was manifestly the duty of all the great Christian nations to aid in its accomplishment. The immediate result of the Conference was the convocation of an International Congress, which met in June, 1877, at the Royal Palace, Brussels, and at which there were present delegates from Belgium, France, the United States, Germany, Austria, the Netherlands, Spain and Switzerland.

This body, of which the King of the Belgians was elected president, assumed the title of the International African Association. It was decided that each nation willing to co-operate in the high mission undertaken should establish a national committee, create an interest in the objects of the Association, collect subscriptions to the general fund, and, in short, promote the success of the undertaking in every legitimate way. It was decided that the flag of the Association should show a blue field with a golden star in the center. The objects of the organization were identical with those previously declared by the preliminary Conference.

In due course of time, national committees were formed in the following countries: Belgium, Germany, France, Austro-Hungary, Italy, the United States, Spain, Switzerland, Russia, Holland and Portugal. Owing to a feeling which may fitly be called hypercautiousness, England elected to remain free from the trammels of all engagements of an international nature, and therefore failed to create a national committee, or to co-operate with the Association in any way. General H. S. Sanford, of Florida, succeeded to the place of Sir Bartle Frere as the representative of the English-speaking races, and Judge Daly, of New York, was the first president of our National Committee. The latter was succeeded by Mr. Latrobe, of Baltimore, one of the founders of Liberia.

Money, to the amount of several hundred thousand francs, flowed into the general treasury—chiefly from the Belgians, be it stated—and in June, 1877, it was decided to commence active operations at once. Accordingly an expedition was sent to Zanzibar to penetrate the interior and establish a chain of stations as far as Lake Tanganyika. This object was successfully accomplished, albeit not without great toil, anxiety, and even tribulation, there being one station under German adminstration, another under the French, while all the remainder must be accredited to the Belgians. Like the stations on the Congo, they are all bases of operations and supplies, and cities of refuge for all sorts of pioneers save the slave-traders.

In 1877, Stanley fought his way down the Congo from near its source to its mouth, 1,562 miles, and reached the ocean on August 12th. The news of his magnificent achievement electrified the world, and his triumphant return to Europe was the signal for a grand outpouring of honors, in which geographers, scientists, statesmen, learned societies, municipalities, kings, and even Houses of Congress, vied with each other as to who should do the weary explorer the highest honor. Never before did medals, imperial portraits, honorary memberships, commanderships, stars and collars fall upon an explorer in such a shower, and forthwith all Europe was agog with excitement over Equatorial Africa.

In November, 1878, a number of " persons of more or less note in the commercial and monetary world, from England, Germany, France, Belgium and Holland " met in the Royal Palace at Brussels. By invitation, Mr. Stanley was present, and furnished the information which constituted the basis of the subsequent deliberations. It was resolved that a fund should be raised with which to send an expedition to the Congo for still further information, and a portion of the capital of £20,000 was subscribed then and there for immediate use. The subscribers to the fund assumed the title of " Comité d' Etudes du Haut Congo," or, " Committee of Study of the Upper Congo."

This body, having for its object the development of a particular region, the Upper Congo, was entirely separate from the African Association, but like the latter it was also international. It elected as its president, Colonel Strauch of the Belgian army. Of course, Mr. Stanley was chosen as the commander of the expedition to the Congo, the great objects of which were to erect commo-

dious and permanent stations along the Congo at
proper distances apart, establish steam communication wherever practicable, acquire a limited amount
of land from the natives by lease or purchase for
the actual needs of the enterprise, and make treaties with the natives all along the river for the promotion and preservation of peace and good will.

The third meeting of the *Comité* was held January 2, 1879, and attended by representatives of
Belgium, Holland, England, France and America.
Mr. Stanley's estimates of expenses and plans of
operations were adopted, and the sums necessary
to carry them out were voted.   By the end of January, the Commander had given orders for all his
materiel,—steamers, lighters, steel whale boats,
portable houses, corrugated iron, wagons, provisions, etc.,—and was on his way to Zanzibar, on
the chartered steamer *Albion*, to enlist a force of
Zanzibaris, including as many members of his
former expedition as could be obtained, for new
service on the Congo.   At Zanzibar, Mr. Stanley was able to be of great service to both the
first and second expeditions of the International
Association, the former of which was then in
Unyanyembe, but presently arrived at Lake Tanganyika, where it established Karema Station.

The *Albion* and Mr. Stanley reached Banana
Point, at the mouth of the Congo, on August 14,

1879—just two years and two days from the time
the explorer saw it at the end of his memorable
voyage through the wilderness.

The twenty-first of August, 1879, was a great
day for Equatorial Africa. It witnessed the inau-
guration of the work on the Congo of the *Comité
d' Etudes du Haut Congo*. It was the beginning
of an era in African history, of a great conquest
by peace and good will. On that date, the expedition steamed out of the Banana harbor and
started up the river.

The expedition consisted of 72 Europeans, 81
Zanzibar natives, and 122 natives of the country.
Its flotilla contained five steamers and launches, a
whale boat and two lighters. On September 27th,
the whole force reached the site of what is now
Vivi, at the head of navigation, and 110 miles from
Banana. A treaty was made, ground cleared, and
Vivi Station built and finished by January 24, 1880.
The next work was building a wagon road fifty-
two miles long, from Vivi around the lower cataracts of the Congo to Isangila, haul the steamers
and small boats, stores and equipage over it, and
when accomplished launch all on the river once
more. This gigantic task was undertaken on February 21, 1880, and completed February 21, 1881.
The difficulties. encountered and overcome will
never be fully appreciated save by those who faced

them. The road was made partly through thick forest, across deep ravines, and over hills of incredible steepness. The amount of labor and successful engineering involved in hauling by hand over this almost impassable road, the huge and heavy steamer sections, engines and other machinery, smaller boats, iron houses, tanks, hardware, provisions, etc., etc., is absolutely inconceivable. Add to this, the diet of beans, goat-meat and sodden bananas, in the muggy atmosphere of the canyon, with the fierce heat from the rocks, the chill, bleak winds blowing up the gorge, and it is no wonder that the death roll for the year included the names of six Europeans, and twenty-two of the natives; or that thirteen more of the white men who joined the force during the year were retired as invalids.

Slowly but surely, like the progress of an ever-victorious army, the expedition, with Stanley at its head, pushed its way up the mighty river, making treaties and purchases of land, building stations at proper intervals, and equipping them with officers, men and stores. As soon as a station was established, on went the main body of the expedition to choose a site and build another still farther in the wilderness. By December 10, 1883, only *one day* behind the schedule time given by the Commander before the *Comité* at Brussels in 1879, the expedition arrived at its farthest point, Stanley Falls, 1,413 miles from the coast, built its last station, and, in one sense, finished its preliminary labors.

Up to that time, the expedition had made over four hundred and fifty treaties with independent African chiefs, built twenty-two stations and one hundred miles of road, placed two steam launches, a whale boat and two large canoes on the waters of the Upper Congo, above Stanley Pool; besides other vessels between the lower cataracts and the Pool. The good will of nearly 1,000,000 natives had been secured along both banks of the river up to Stanley Falls. The white chiefs of the expedition had entered into the bonds of blood-brother-hood with the very natives who fiercely fought Stanley on his way down the river in 1877. The foundations of a grand structure had been success-fully laid, and the next step was a political one.

In the course of time, the International African Association assumed the direction of affairs in the Congo Free State, and the Committee of Study of the Upper Congo was superseded by the Com-mittee of the International Association of the Congo. The grand work so auspiciously begun by the Committee of Study was continued on the same plan with precisely the same machinery, but under a different name and higher patronage.

Portugal claimed the territory to the south of
that occupied by the *Comité d' Etudes du Haut
Congo*, and France put in a claim for what lay
north of it.   No boundaries had been determined,
and the flag of the Association was as yet wholly
unrecognized by the great nations.

As the preliminary work of the expedition ap-
proached a successful termination, it became evi-
dent that something must be done to make the
administration of the new state secure against en-
croachment from without; to define its rights;
legalize its acts, and so enable it to become self-
supporting.   During the first five or six years of
the work, the King of the Belgians contributed
£200,000 annually (a million dollars a year, if you
please!) toward its support, and even at present its
chief source of support is the £40,000 annual en-
dowment derived from the same munificent source.

Seeing that the great nations were too indifferent to his great undertaking to further its political
advancement without being asked, His Majesty
was compelled to apply to the various governments
of Europe and America for the recognition which
should have been accorded unasked.

The whole political history of the founding of
the Congo Free State "officially" is little more
than an exposition of the petty meanness and char-
latanry which sometimes characterize great nations

when dealing with each other, or with helpless in-
feriors. Those nations of Europe which have ever
been most greedy and unscrupulous, even to the
point of outrage itself, sometimes, in seizing territory whenever any is found rich enough and sufficiently exposed;—those nations whose colonies
levy the highest duties on imports, were the very
ones which most persistently refused to recognize
the independent nationality of the Congo Free
State; nor would they yield even then, save on the
condition that they should make its laws, and provide for the absolute freedom of commerce, beyond a peradventure. Thanks to the eternal fires
of jealousy burning in the hearts of the great
nations, and the dog-in-the-manger policy which
resulted therefrom, the Congo Free State came
into the world a hopeless cripple, without visible
means of support. But I must not anticipate.

The first blow struck at the Free State was by
Earl Granville in behalf of Great Britain. For
nearly fifty years the British Government, through
its ministers, had consistently and persistently refused to recognize the claims of Portugal to the
Congo region of West Africa; but in consequence
of negotiations entered upon in 1882 and concluded
in February, 1884, a treaty was formulated between
those two countries which completely reversed the
old order of things. Great Britain recognized the

right of Portugal to the Lower Congo, thus de-
nying the right of the Free State to any seaport
whatever!

As might have been expected, this treaty
aroused a storm of indignation in Europe, and
even in England outside of the foreign office.
The most powerful protest against it came from
the United States, through the instrumentality of
Gen. Sanford. After an investigation of all the
facts bearing on the case, the Senate on April 10,
1884, passed a resolution authorizing the President
to formally recognize the flag of the International
African Association as that of a governing power
on the Congo. Thus, as in the case of the Territory of Sarawak, Borneo, were we the first to
recognize the independence of the new State. Of
this act, Mr. Stanley declares:

"The recognition of the United States was the
birth unto new life of the Association, seriously
menaced as its existence was by opposing interests
and ambitions; and the following of this example
by the European powers has affirmed and secured
its place among Sovereign States. This act, the
result of the well-considered judgment of the
American statesmen, was greatly criticised abroad,
as was the participation of the United States in the
Berlin Conference, to which it led up, by the press

of America. It was an act well worthy of the
Great Republic."

Not only did a portion of the American press
raise an outcry against the participation of our government in the Berlin Conference, but even Congress, and finally the President himself, shared
the fright at the great national bugaboo, Entangling Alliance. For a time, the forces of the
hypercautious promised to place our representatives in an exceedingly painful position, and ourselves in a very ridiculous light; but the storm
which threatened finally subsided with but slight
casualties. But the opposition aroused emphasized
once more the fact that our wise policy of non-in-
terference has degenerated into a silly fear to take
a political step in any direction beyond our own
borders. Public duty looks in but one direction,
inward, and we have become so wedded to the
petty details of government, that we utterly ignore
all great tasks, even the building of adequate coast
defenses.

Even in the presentation of as great a moral issue as the suppression of the liquor traffic on the
Congo, there is all manner of evil to dread from
our policy of masterly inactivity abroad, and the
national bugaboo. When the question of active
interference in this matter is presented to the people and their representatives, and they are called

upon to take decisive action in behalf of people we never saw, who are not American citizens, and of no benefit to us *financially*, we will await the result with hope tempered by fear.

The action of the British Foreign Office in the conclusion of the notorious Anglo-Portuguese treaty in defiance of the wishes of the people, was another instance of the abuse of power which is common in all monarchies. "The British Chambers of Commerce, notably those of Manchester, Liverpool and Glasgow, resolutely opposed the treaty concluded with Portugal, but with all the strenuous opposition maintained to it in commercial circles and in the House of Commons, had not the Royal Founder of the Association obtained the assistance of the German Chancellor and the sympathies of the French Government, it is doubtful whether anything done in England would have succeeded in averting the effectual seal being put upon enterprise in the Congo basin." (*Stanley.*)

For once national selfishness led to a result which was partly for good. Bismarck and France refused to recognize the terms of the treaty, and it fell to the ground. Had it been carried into effect, it would have had a most disastrous effect upon German and French commerce on the Congo. Seeing that German commercial interests in the Congo Free State were in jeopardy, Prince Bis-

marck wrote to the French Government propos-
ing a Conference on the subject, to which should
be invited representatives from all other nations
whose interests were likely to be affected.

At this point, it is well to note one pertinent
fact. This Conference was proposed, not for the
benefit of the Congo Free State, or the people, but
to secure the absolute freedom of commerce (*i. e.*,
freedom from import duties) for German subjects,
even though it left the administration of the Free
State *absolutely without an income.* In the very
conception of the plan for a Conference, it was
agreed between Mr. Ferry and the German Am-
bassador at Paris that the Congo and the Niger
should be made free to all flags. In the invitation
to the Conference which Mr. Frelinghuysen received from the German minister at Washington,
on October 10, 1884, the free navigation clause is
the first one set forth.

Invitations to participate in the Berlin West
African Conference were finally extended to fourteen nations, and on November 15, 1884, the various representatives, chiefly ministers and ambas-
sadors, met at Berlin and chose Prince Bismarck
for their president. The following are the names
of the Powers participating, and the chief representatives of each:

Belgium, Count Van der Straten and Baron Lambermont.

Germany, Prince Bismarck and Count Hatzfeldt; Dr. Busch and Herr Henry de Kusserow.

France, Baron de Courcel.

United States, Hon. John A. Kasson and Gen. H. S. Sanford.

England, Sir Edward B. Malet.

Austria, Count Széchenyi.

Italy, Count de Launay.

The Netherlands, Le Jonkheer Van der Hoeven.

Denmark, M. Emile de Vind.

Spain, Count de Benomar.

Portugal, Marquis de Penafiel and Senor A. de Serpa Pimentel.

Russia, Count Kapnist.

Sweden and Norway, Baron Bildt.

Turkey, Said Pacha.

Of the seventeen delegates and experts who formed the suites of these high representatives, I will pause to mention only four: Herr Adolphe Woerman, of Hamburg, shipper of poisonous brandy of the worst quality (according to his own confession) to the Congo natives; Mr. A. D. Bloeme, manager of eighty trading "factories" in West Africa; Col. Strauch, President of the *Comité d'Etudes du Haut Congo*, and Mr. Henry M. Stanley, who needs neither title nor introduction.

The sitting of the Conference was a very long one, lasting from November 15, 1884, to February 26, 1885, but its deliberations can be summed up in a very few words.

With the Conference as a whole, the Alpha and Omega of its deliberations were for securing forever, beyond a peradventure or the possibility of a doubt, the absolute freedom of commerce to the flags of all nations in the basins of the Congo and the Lower Niger. In the General Act of the Conference, the official residuum of all the deliberations, declarations, protocols and annexes, this declaration was driven home and clinched in the most positive and emphatic manner.

For example: Article I. declares that "The trade of all nations shall be entirely free." Article II., "That goods imported shall pay no taxes except for the necessary expenses of trade," and Article IV., that "Goods imported shall remain free of all charges for entry and transit." All of which are simply three different forms for the declaration of the same thing. It merely serves to show the absurd earnestness of the Conference in securing that one all-precious privilege, the absolute freedom of trade.

Article VI. relates to the "Protection of the natives, to missionaries and travelers, and to religious liberty." Of the whole thirty-three articles relating to the regions mentioned,—the Congo and Lower Niger valleys,—twenty-eight relate to trade, three to the neutrality of the country, and two to the welfare of the natives. In the whole Act, there is not even one article in the interest of the International Association or the Government of the Congo Free State; the development of the country on a broad and liberal plan, or the making of any improvements whatever, save those by which trade may be facilitated as, for example, the building of wharves, ware-houses and light-houses.

The General Act of the Berlin Conference covers eighteen printed pages, contains six chapters and thirty-eight articles, but without doing the slightest violence to the reader's patience, I can reproduce here every word of the text which is in any way calculated to promote the welfare of the African people, or the great objects of the International Association. This high and puissant instrument, this General Act of International Selfishness and Inhumanity begins most piously,

" *In the Name of Almighty God.*"

Thirty-one articles are solely in the interests of commerce and free navigation; two relate to the conditions which must govern future annexations of African territory; three are general provisions for the acceptance of the Act, and two refer in a

general and wholly desultory way to the interests
of the people.

Here they are in full:

"*Article VI. Provisions Relative to the Protection of the Natives, to Missionaries and Travelers,
and to Religious Liberty.*

"All the powers exercising sovereign rights, or
having influence in said territories, undertake to
watch over the preservation of the native races,
and the amelioration of the moral and material
conditions of their existence, and to co-operate in
the suppression of slavery, and above all, of the
slave trade; they will protect and encourage without distinction of nationality or creed, all institu-
tions and enterprises—religious, scientific or charitable—established and organized for these objects,
or tending to educate the natives and lead them to
understand and appreciate the advantages of civilization. Christian missionaries, men of science,
explorers, and their escorts and collections, to be
equally the object of special protection. Liberty
of conscience and religious toleration are expressly
guaranteed to the natives as well as to inhabitants
and foreigners. The free and possible exercise of
every creed, the right to erect religious buildings
and to organize missions belonging to every
creed, shall be subject to no restriction or impedi-
ment whatsoever."

"*Article IX. Declaration Concerning the Slave Trade.*

"In conformity with the principles of the right of nations as recognized by the signatory Powers, the slave trade being forbidden, and operations which on land or sea supply slaves for the trade being equally held to be forbidden, the Powers which exercise, or will exercise, rights of sovereignty or influence in the territories forming the basin of the Congo declare that these territories shall serve neither for the place of sale nor the way of transit for the traffic in slaves of any race whatsoever. Each of the Powers undertakes to employ every means that it can to put an end to the trade and to punish those who engage in it."

In the whole of this high and mighty Act, there is not the slightest mention of any restriction on the trade in intoxicating liquors, or the promotion of temperance, or of any method or system whatsoever by which the condition of the people should be benefited in any way. In the matter of free trade, however, there are pages upon pages of details. So far as the improvement of the condition of the African people was concerned, or the interests of the Congo Free State furthered, the Conference might just as well have never been held. Judged by the result, we may truthfully say that it was a Conference for trade only, and it

is simply disgraceful that the spirit of trade, gain,
pecuniary advantage, and international greed
should have so completely monopolized the deliberations of the Conference and the declarations
of the Act. "In the name of Almighty God" we
want free trade in Africa, says the Act, and we
are going to have it.

Not a single dollar is provided for "the amelioration of the condition of the natives," not a single individual is appointed for that purpose, not a
single step taken, nor even proposed, for the suppression of the slave trade, that had not already
been taken by the Powers years and years ago, in
the Congress of Vienna as far back as 1815. Even
Portugal has declared against the slave trade, officially, although the infernal traffic still goes on
openly and above board in her African territory.
Steps enough were taken to promote and protect
the interests of commerce, even though it should
be commerce in poisonous brandy and alcohol,
imported by the ship-load; but not a single step
was taken to protect the morals of the natives,
much less to promote their material welfare.

But, it may be replied, the government of the
Congo Free State can itself pass laws for the protection of the people. Let me tell you it can do no
such thing in regard to the traffic in liquor. The
importation and sale of brandy, rum, gin, whisky

and alcohol is "trade," and the Great Powers
(great in greediness) have decreed in the strong-
est terms that trade shall be *absolutely free* in that
region. Rum has the right of way by international edict, and the International Association cannot stop the sale of a single bottle of it without
the consent of the Powers. If the opium growers
of India want to send opium to the Congo and
teach all the natives to use it, they can do so. It
is "trade," it is "commerce," and they are absolutely free, you know. You can perpetrate any
crime you wish over there, provided you do it in
the sacred name of trade. Is this nonsense? Is
it preposterous and absurd? If you think so, pray
turn at once to the next chapter.

In conclusion it may be stated that the example
of the United States, in recognizing the flag of
the International Association as that of an independent power, was finally followed by about all
the European nations. Treaties and declarations
defining intentions, rights and territorial boundaries were formally concluded between the Association and the Great Powers, and the flag of the
Association was thus officially recognized by the
following nations in the order named:

United States, April 22, 1884; Germany, November 8th; England, December 16th; Belgium,
December 23d; the Netherlands, December 27th;

France, February 5, 1885; and Portugal, February 14th.

Thus was the Congo Free State accorded a place in the family of nations. Its territory embraced the greater portion of the country drained by the Congo and its tributaries, nearly one million square miles, with a population estimated at forty-three millions.

The King of the Belgians appointed Sir Francis de Winton, an Englishman, the first Governor-General of the Free State, and in the spring of 1885 the newly-formed government assumed control of the port of Banana, and others on the Lower Congo. From whence the Free State is to derive a sufficient revenue for its support, on a scale at all proportionate to the beginning that was made for it by the King of the Belgians, is a question yet to be answered. The notorious Act of the Conference expressly declares (Article XIV.) that on commerce "There shall not be established any tolls, marine or river, based on the fact of navigation alone, nor shall any duty be imposed on the merchandise on board the vessels. Such taxes and duties only shall be levied as are of the character of remuneration for services rendered to said navigation. That is to say,

" 1. Taxes of the port for the actual use of certain local establishments, such as wharves, warehouses, etc.

" 2. Pilotage dues on sections of the river, or where it appears necessary to establish stations of certified pilots.

"3. Dues in respect to the technical and administrative expenses, imposed in the general interest of the navigation, and comprising light-house, beacon and buoyage dues."

Set forth in plain English, without any euphemism, the above article says, " We will enter in, even to the uttermost parts of the territory opened up at the expense of life and treasure on the part of the International Association. We will enjoy the fruits of your labors, but the laborer is not worthy of his hire, and we will pay you nothing for the privilege of traveling with our goods over the roads you have made, and through the territories you have subdued by costly acts of peace and good will. You have got to protect us, and keep the country quiet, but the privilege of protecting wealthy and enterprising subjects of powerful nations must be your only reward. We have a right to compete with you in everything you undertake that has money in it, but everything that is done *pro bono publico* must be done by you. You must labor, and we must be allowed to reap the fruit of it. Virtue is its own reward. Go to."

This is the doctrine of meanness. Almost without exception the colonies of the powers who drafted that infamous Act charge import duties, and some of them most shamelessly, too, as a means of revenue for the support of their colonial governments. By this means, as trade increases, great public improvements are rendered possible, and the people are benefited. Roads are made, insurrections are put down, slavery suppressed, schools, markets and hospitals are built, industries fostered, and the people protected. It is only a law of common decency that trade should be made to support the government which opens the way for it, and protects it. The refusal to allow the levy of any import or export duties in the Congo Free State was an act of international meanness and injustice. Such truculence to the greedy demands of trade falls not far short of pusillanimity.

CHAPTER IV.

FREE RUM AND WHOLESALE DRUNKENNESS ON THE CONGO.

The Berlin Conference decreed that the commerce of all nations should be absolutely free in the basins of the Congo and the Niger. Indeed, besides this, the Conference did little else worth mentioning for the Congo Free State. It was merely a commercial barter, in which the only factor was hard cash. Since no nation could hope to gain any special advantage in the face of so many rivals, it was mutually agreed that the Congo black was the legitimate prey of all, and all should have *carte-blanche* to prey upon him, free of charge, in any manner whatsoever. Not a single safeguard was thrown around him; not a single step was taken for his benefit, and what is still worse, nothing was done to prevent his being sunk even lower than he is.

In all the various countries whose representatives participated in that Conference, the wild animals, the birds and the fishes are, by law, protected from destruction, even for food. In some countries it is against the law to shoot even a bird of prey. In our own country a perfect storm of indignation has been raised against the destruction of birds for millinery purposes. It matters not whether they are singing birds or not; wanton and wholesale destruction is a crime, even though lovely woman herself demands the spoil.

But with the African the case is different. We do not see him, and we feel no personal interest in him, for the very selfish reason that he cannot do anything for us. Therefore Christendom says to the keen-eyed and enterprising trader, "There he is, your lawful prey; up and at him, and put money in thy purse. Sell him anything you please, provided you can sell it at a profit. I care not what becomes of him. Am I my brother's keeper?"

We protect our deer and grouse, and even our sparrows; but is he not "of greater value than many sparrows"?

Perhaps there are those who will say that all this is cant; sentiment; much ado about nothing. Let me tell you, it is nothing of the sort. I offer nothing but hard facts and plain figures, and I challenge the champions of intemperance to disprove them. They loom up like a hideous black mountain on a plain, and all the rum makers and friends of rum in Christendom cannot hide them from view. Those who do not wish to encounter

them can go around them,—until the judgment
day,—but their dark shadows will fall on the indifferent ones, whether they will or not. ·

What is all this outcry about? Why, simply
this: By reason of the total absence of restrain-
ing laws heretofore, and the special privilege
granted by the General Act of the Berlin Conference, the traders of Holland, Germany, Portugal,
the United States, France and England, are pouring cheap and deadly liquor into Africa by the
ship-load. The natives have developed an appe-
tite for it almost beyond the power of belief, and
it is used for currency instead of money. In fact,
gin is the lever by which Africa is being "opened
up." Let me quote a few travelers on the subject;
men who saw what they relate.

Shortly before the convening of the Berlin
Conference our Secretary of State sent Mr. N. P.
Tisdel to the Congo as a special diplomatic agent,
to examine the country and its inhabitants, and
report upon both. Mr. Tisdel arrived in Banana
early in December, 1884, and with a special caravan journeyed up to and around Stanley Pool,
arriving at Banana again on March 20, 1885.
His report to the Department of State appears in
the Consular Report for July and August, 1885,—
Nos. 54 and 55. The report deals strictly with

facts bearing on the commercial prospects of the region visited. Here are a few of them:

"Gold, silver, or paper money is wholly unknown, the currency of the country being gin, glass beads, brass rods, red cotton handkerchiefs, trade cloth, powder and flint-lock guns. * * * Of this variegated currency, gin is the most valuable; indeed, it may be truly said that 'it is worth its weight in gold.' * * * Goats and fowls they (the natives) rarely ever eat, reserving them for trade; and oftentimes they send them hundreds of miles to exchange them for gin or powder."

"Unfortunately, a few bottles of trade-gin will go much farther in trade with the natives than *ten times its value in cloth;* and it often happens that traders are compelled to return to the coast without having accomplished a trade, because the natives insist upon having GIN, while the trader was supplied with cloth alone. A native man can be induced to work at a "factory" for one or two days at a time upon the assurance that he can, at the expiration of that time, have a bottle or two of gin; while, if you offer him a piece of cloth, it is doubtful if he would work at all. * * * The men lounge about, drinking, gossiping, fighting or hunting, as it may suit their tastes."

Notwithstanding the assertions of the traders, of Mr. Tisdel, and even Mr. Stanley himself, that

it is utterly impossible to trade with the natives
without rum or gin, we have now most positive
proof that a large and profitable business can be
done without the agency of a single drop of liquor.
There is one English trading company, having
twelve stations between the coast and the region
of the great lakes, which finds it not only possible
but profitable to get along without poisoning or
debauching the natives. Says the London *Times:*

"During the eight years in which the company
has extended the ramifications of its trade over
this immense distance, it has proved that it is possible to trade in India rubber, wax, oilseeds and
ivory to an enormous amount without defiling the
list of their barter goods with a single keg of
trade-rum, or the all-representative 'square-face'
of the West Coast trade. It is something to have
established proof before us that it is not necessary
to carry ruin and desolation, headed up in Hamburg casks and Dutch gin bottles, to a new
country, before you can hope to see tusks and
dividends. The Messrs. Moir, who are entrusted
with the concerns of the company, testify that they
have already exported 40,815 pounds of ivory,
and not imported a glass of spirits."

All honor to this company and the Messrs.
Moir! It is really inspiring to know that at least
one trading company is animated by a truly human

and Christian spirit; and such positive proof that rum is *not* absolutely necessary to profitable trade in Africa, and that the trader *can* get along very well without it, is of priceless value to us at this time.

Speaking of Angola, the Portuguese territory adjoining the Free State on the south, Mr. Tisdel says, "There are no manufactories in the country *excepting for rum*."

Here is a bit of testimony which speaks volumes for what is being done on the Niger. It is what Joseph Thompson saw "Up the Niger," as related in *Good Words* for January, 1886:

"At each port of call, one becomes bewildered in watching the discharge of thousands of cases of gin, hundreds of demijohns of rum, box upon box of guns, untold kegs of gunpowder and myriads of clay pipes, while it seems as if only by accident a stray bale of cloth went over the side."

Now look upon this picture and see what New England is doing to help the cause along. The superintendent of Lutheran missions in West Africa writes as follows:

"The vilest liquors imaginable are being poured into Africa in shiploads from almost every quarter of the civilized world. On one small vessel, in which myself and wife were the only passengers,

there were in the hold over 100,000 gallons of New
England rum, which sold on the coast for $1 a
gallon in exchange for palm-oil, rubber, camwood,
and other products common to the country. I have
seen landed from one steamer, at a single port, 10,-
000 cases of gin, each containing twelve three-
pint bottles."

The next witness shall be no less a man than
the founder of the Congo Free State. In Stanley's
"Congo," Vol. I, p. 193, he writes as follows:

" Gin is used as currency. * * * Gin and
rum are also largely consumed as grog by our native workmen. We dilute both largely, but we
are compelled to serve it out both morning and
evening. A stoppage of this would be followed
by a cessation of work. It is ' custom'; custom is
despotic, and we are too weak and too new in the
country to rebel against custom. If we resist custom we shall be abandoned. Every visitor to our
camp on this part of the Congo [the Lower], if
he has a palaver with us, must first receive a small
glass of rum or gin. A chief receives a bottleful,
which he distributes teaspoonful by teaspoonful
among his followers. This is the Lower Congo
idea of ' an all-around drink.' I see by the returns of the station chief that we consume 125
gallons of rum monthly, by distributing grog

rations and native demands for it in lieu of a portion of their wages."

I have reserved the most important testimony
until the last. It is that of Dr. A. Sims, chief of
the Livingstone Inland Congo Mission, who was
the first missionary to navigate the waters of the
Upper Congo, and has lately returned to this country after four years' work in that deadly climate.
In a recent letter to the writer he furnishes the
following facts:

" Besides the giving of rum in payment for
goods or food supplies, it is employed in a wholesale way as presents. The traders keep their ' run-
ners ' on the roads frequented by natives, whom
they bribe with liquor to trade only with their
masters. The moment natives with produce ar-
rive in a merchant's yard, they are liquored all
round. * * * All contract dues, and ground-
rents are made payable more than half, or, as is
often the case, wholly in demijohns of rum and
cases of gin. In this the Congo Free State has
followed the example set by the merchants. Rum
is now carried into the far interior by natives and
retailed at a profit. At my house, 325 miles in the
interior, a bottle of Rotterdam gin has been offered to me at 16 cents (eight brass rods), and a
demijohn at $3. At that place caravans of Bateké
and Bakongo continually passed, of which twenty-

five men out of every hundred would be loaded
with intoxicating drinks. From such sources of
supply I have seen many natives and soldiers of
the State become drunk immediately upon the
arrival of a caravan. It is pretty certain that 50
per cent of the returned commerce account of the
natives who live near the trading-houses is given
to them in liquor. At Stanley Pool not more than
25 per cent of the value of their goods goes back
to them in liquor, but that is because of the distance. Were they living near a trader they would
be hopelessly drunken. It is a sad thought that
where five years ago liquor was unknown and
never asked for, the natives now beg for it, and
nothing else can better ingratiate one into their
favor. As for the kings near the seaside trading-
houses, intoxication is about their normal condition.
When I was assisting to ·conduct a mission at
Banana, the port of the Congo, it was difficult to
get the natives to assemble in a sober state on Sab-
bath morning."

Is this testimony enough for the present? If not,
the next chapter will set forth a few figures to
throw light upon the subject from another direction.
One word more, however, as to the quality of the
rum supplied. We shall presently consider the
quantity also.

Those who read the New York *Tribune* of January 24, 1886, must have noticed the following bit of telegraphic news from Berlin, dated the previous day:

"In the discussion in the Reichstag on the Cameroon credits, Herren Windthorst, Richter and Stoecker charged Herr Woerman, deputy for Hamburg, and the chief of a large exporting house, with sending poisonous brandy to the negroes in Africa. Herr Woerman acknowledged that the charge was partially true. He said, however, that he had never sent bad brandy to any of the German colonies, but to the French colonies. To these he had shipped rum of the worst quality."

The attention of French statesmen is particularly invited to this highly conscientious discrimination on the part of Herr Woerman. He cannot bear the thought of debauching the savage subjects of his own government, but who cares for Johnny Crapaud's blacks? Give them the worst stuff in the shop. If it kills them off like flies no matter,—or rather so much the better, for the Frenchman loses by it. Long live the King, and God bless the Fatherland!

Through the kindness of our Secretary of State and our diplomatic service in Europe, I have been placed in possession of many important facts bearing on the exportation of intoxicating liquors to Africa.

In regard to the liquor supply on the Congo, Mr. D. Eckstein, U. S. Consul at Amsterdam, reports the following information, gleaned by him from a most trustworthy source:

" On the Congo, the Germans and Belgians spoil the liquor business by selling at wretchedly low prices. * * * Eatables from Europe the natives do not want; clothing, hardly; finances to only a small extent; but *gin* and *rum* they do want sorely, and it is provided for them, often *in the most miserable form of adulterated stuff*."

I have already pointed out the fact that the natives of Africa wherever liquor is introduced among them, have developed a passionate craving for it that is almost without a parallel. Knowing but little of the horde of evils that follow in the train of drunkenness, caring nothing for the future, and fearing no evils they are unacquainted with, the African savage thinks only of the pleasure of getting drunk. When sober, he feels no remorse of conscience, for he is not conscious of having done wrong. Did not the white man make and furnish the rum? The white man not only sells it to him, but he drinks it himself. Why should he not do as does the white man, who knows everything? He says to himself, " The black man has few pleasures, and the greatest of them is getting drunk on fire-water. I have plenty of palm-oil, and fire-water is cheap; therefore why should I not get drunk every day?"

The seed has been planted, and by the hands of enlightened statesmen and traders, in the blazing light of the nineteenth century. What shall the harvest be?

We know, alas! too well, what intemperance is doing to-day in our own land; aye, in our own city, in our own street. It breeds more curses than all the other scourges of the earth put together. Even in the temperate zone, where man attains his highest development, and is fitted to resist longest the effects of disease or debauchery, the graves of the drunkards are as the sands of the sea. But witness the still more deadly effects of intemperance in the deadlier climate of the Congo. The following is from Stanley's "Congo:"

" The very atmosphere [of the Congo Free State] seems to be fatally hostile to the physique of men who pin their faith to whisky, gin and brandy. They invariably succumb, and are a constant source of expense. Even if they are not finally buried out of sight, and out of memory, they are so utterly helpless, diseases germinate with such frightful rapidity, symptoms of insanity are numerous; and, with mind vacant and body semi-paralyzed,

they are hurried homeward to make room for
more valuable substitutes."

" The indigenous races of the free zone must
be sober," says Count Van der Straten, " or soon
cease to exist. The negro does not yield physically to drunkenness; he succumbs morally.   If
the powers do not save him from this vice, they
will make of him *a monster who will destroy the
work of the Conference.*"

If the condition of the West African savage
was deplorably, almost hopelessly, low before
drunkenness was added to his load of ignorance
and vice, what must it be now? Why, some
authorities even despaired of the black man's future before the rivers of rum were set aflow.
Here is the calm opinion of J. J. Monteiro formed
by " many years of travel and exploration in
West Africa."

" I do not believe, and I fearlessly assert, that
there is hardly such a thing possible as the sincere
conversion of a single negro to Christianity whilst
in Africa, and under the powerful influence of
his fellows. No progress will be made in the
condition of the negro so long as the idea prevails
that he can be reasoned out of his ignorance and
prejudices, and his belief in fetish, or that he is the
equal of the white man; in fact, he must remain
the same as he is now, until we learn to know him

properly, and what he really is." (*Angola and the River Congo. p. 44.*)

If this was true, or even partly .true of the negro before the wholesale introduction of drunkenness (it was written in 1876), how much harder must be the task of the missionary now than it was then! What an incalculable amount of labor, lives and treasure the Christian Church might have saved by barring the doors of Africa at the right time against alcohol! Now a world of mischief is already done. A little longer and it will be too late to accomplish anything on a grand scale. It is still possible to shut liquor out of Africa, or out of the Congo Free State at all events, *provided* the effort is made in force, and in the right direction. Oh, ye missionaries! how much longer will you strive to save the blasted tree by doctoring its leaves, while the poison is being poured around its roots!

Oh, ye churches! Why do you blindly persist in lavishing your good works upon a handful of individuals, when it lies in your power to confer a tremendous blessing upon the whole mass, by one master-stroke, and pave the way to the conversion of a million of sober savages, instead of the thousand reclaimed drunkards you might otherwise expect! Your missionaries and your funds are all needed in the great campaign you should make in this country and in Europe in behalf of temperance in Africa, in general, and in the Congo Free State in particular. Why fritter away great resources in philanthropic work on a small scale, when the same capital could be made to yield a blessing of the first magnitude to *fifty millions of people?* The churches and the friends of temperance possess ample power to bring about the closing of every West African port against intoxicating liquor, *if* they but choose to exercise it, and *carry the war into Africa.* With one-half the money that will be spent this year by the churches, for Africa, and with the services of one-half the evangelists who will spend their time there, almost any good leader could conduct a campaign which would result in the legislation necessary to stop that infernal traffic, for a long period, to say the least. *At present,* the task is simple, and if undertaken in the right way its accomplishment is not only possible but certain. Statesmen are not dead to all sense of human sympathy, or strangers to all motives of philanthropy. The first year's history of the Congo Free State has proved that the work of the Conference at Berlin, so far as the people's welfare was concerned, was a serious mistake. The error was a double one, of both commission and omission, but its rectification is both simple and easy.

There should be another Conference of the Powers, at once, in behalf of temperance in Africa, in which the good of the people should be the keynote of all deliberations. The moral and material welfare of fifty millions of savages is most certainly of sufficient importance to warrant the assembling of another conference; and if called to-morrow it could not assemble a day too soon for the crying needs of the people of Africa.

CHAPTER V.

WHERE THE POISON COMES FROM.

As to the parties actually engaged in the exportation of intoxicating liquors to West Africa and the Congo Free State in particular, it is impossible to name all, or even any but the largest companies. Mr. Tisdel reports the following as being old-established houses, each with many branches and with its own line of steamers and sailing vessels:

The Dutch-African Trading Company, of Rotterdam.

Hatton and Cookson, of Liverpool.

The Congo and Central African Company, of Liverpool.

The Hamburg-African Company, of Hamburg.

Daumas, Béraud & Co., of Paris.

After these come the newer firms of

The New African Commercial Association.

Hendrick Muller & Co.

The Handels Compagnie " Mozambique,"
all of Rotterdam.

Mr. Tisdel's report contains this illustration of the extent of the business done by one of these

companies, and the reader can form his own estimate of the capital involved:

" The Dutch-African Trading Company of
Rotterdam has fifty-three " factories" or stations,
the principal one being at Banana Point, where
the manager for the Company resides. The fifty-
two remaining "factories" are scattered from
Loango, in latitude 4° 40′ S., to Benguela, in latitude 13° 40′ S., and to the interior about 100 miles,
the limit of the lowland. On the Congo River,
proper, they have only seven stations, and with
two exceptions these are unimportant, when com-
pared with many of the other stations along the
coast and lower river. By this method, the different posts are kept supplied with the articles required by the natives, and the products of the
surrounding country are gathered in small
lots and transported to Banana, where pack-
ages are prepared for shipment to Europe,
whence they are shipped in steamers belonging
to the company. The same plan is adopted by
English, German and French companies, hence
their independence and ability to control the trade
of the lower country. * * * There are also
several Portuguese " factories " in the lower river
(Congo), the headquarters, however, being in
Ambriz, or St. Paul de Loando. There are no
Portuguese houses between the Congo and Am-

briz, nor anywhere in the interior, excepting
Banana and Noki."

Although I do not pretend to be able to state
fully the sources from which the rum traffic in
Africa is supplied, I can, at least, throw some light
on the subject. The devil's agents are as shrewd
as himself, and they do their very utmost to con-
ceal their operations. But do not flatter them for
a moment by supposing that shame is their motive
for concealment.. Not at all. Their slowness
about coming forward with facts is purely due to
business caution, and the fear that news of their
real profits in the liquor traffic would bring too
many rival firms around them. But for this ever-
present fear, and the natural yearning for monop-
oly, it might be possible to get some facts about
trade of an African trading company. As it is,
however, it is doubtful if even the tortures of the
Spanish Inquisition could persuade an exporter to
tell how much bad liquor he sends to the Congo
each year. Mr. Tisdel frankly declares his utter
inability to elicit any information whatever regarding imports from any of the trading houses on the
Congo, and he states that inquiries are always po-
litely referred to the home office. Mr. Eckstein,
of Amsterdam, reports that a friend of his en-
deavored to obtain from a near relative, who is a
director of an African trading company, some

accurate information touching the importation of
liquors, but

"His relative at Rotterdam is disinclined to com-
municate any information relating to his exports of
spirituous liquors to the Congo, or elsewhere in
Africa, or *any other information* on the subject.
Application for such information is continually being made to him by different parties."

Of course not. No merchant is going to give
information when it is likely to injure his business.
But, thanks to the Department of State, and to
Consul Eckstein, I am able to lay before my reader
a full statement of the total exportations of liquors
from the Netherlands to Africa during the last
three years.

INTOXICATING LIQUORS EXPORTED FROM THE
NETHERLANDS TO AFRICA.

WHITHER EXPORTED.	1883 LITERS	1884 LITERS	1885 LITERS
Africa, East Coast...............	217,339	7,479	20,341
Africa, Wes. Coast	3,214,312	4,636,040	4,119,553
Algiers		1,377	689
Egypt..........		14,595	19,592
Total Liters..................	3,431,651	4,659,491	4,160,675
or Gallons..................	906,556	1,230,921	1,099,146

Consul Eckstein states, "that all exporters clear
their goods, spirits, etc., for the 'West Coast of
Africa,' a vague distinction, which is probably
done to hide their real destination—the Congo, in
most cases."

Here is what enlightened New England is doing to help along the cause of poor humanity.

Mr. L. Edwin Dudley, Secretary of the Citizens' Law and Order League, very kindly procured for me from the Collector of the port of Boston the following statement of the quantity of rum exported from that port to Africa, during the fiscal year ending June 30, 1886.

```
In July, 1885, there were shipped................155,821 Gallons
"  Oct.,   "       "       .................145,147    "
"  Jan ,  1886,    "       .................133,820    "
"  Feb.,   "       "       .................121,642    "
"  June,   "       "       .................181,220    ".

    Making a total of .........................737,650 Gallons
```

Nearly 6,000,000 pint bottles of rum, or enough if laid end to end in a straight line touching each other, to reach from Washington to Chicago! Just how much of the same stuff has gone from other ports of ours remains to be ascertained.

England's contribution toward the promotion of drunkenness in Africa, in the year 1885, was as below:

SPIRITUOUS LIQUORS EXPORTED FROM GREAT BRITAIN TO AFRICA IN 1885.

	Gallons	Value
To British Colonies in West Africa	46,233	£ 9,964
To British Colonies in South Africa	86,511	" 38,171
To other Colonies in West Africa	178,640	" 28,447
Total,	311,384	£276,582

France, also, has been guilty, but not to such an extent as some of her neighbors. According to her own official report, she ships a goodly quantity of raw spirits (*"alcool pur"*), or alcohol of great strength, with which a skillful manipulator can make almost any kind of common fire-water. During the year 1885, the exportations of *"Eau-de-vie (alcool pur)"* to the West Coast of Africa, amounted to 17,954 Hectoliters (=396,484 gallons) and to Senegal, (Fr.) the *"Liquers"* amounted to 73,714 Liters, or 19,460 gallons, making a total of 405,944 gallons of intoxicating liquors sent to West Africa from France.

If you have already been appalled by the enormous quantity of liquor sent to the negroes of Africa from the Netherlands, the United States, France and England, what will you say of the showing made by Germany? The amounts seem almost incredible, but they are taken from the official sources in Hamburg, by Mr. Wm. W. Lang, U. S. Consul, and are undoubtedly correct.

OFFICIAL STATEMENT OF THE QUANTITY OF IN-
TOXICATING LIQUORS EXPORTED FROM HAM-
BURG TO THE CONGO AND OTHER PARTS OF
AFRICA DURING TWO YEARS.

(In quantities of 100 Kilograms, gross.)

KIND.	1884	1885
Cognac	40,200 Kgs.	19,'00
Rum	11,154,900 "	10,835,600
Alcohol	1,049,800 "	721,800
Gin	22,252,900 "	20,799,500
Cordials, etc.	681,200 "	710,500
	35,139,000 Kgs.	33,086,800 Kgs. or 7,823,042 net gals.

Excepting from Spain and Portugal, the returns are about all in; enough at least for the present. Let us add the totals together and see what they amount to.

Total shipments of intoxicating liquor to the Natives of Africa, in one year, from five countries:

From the Netherlands	1,099,146	Gallons
" United States	737,650	"
" Great Britain	311,384	"
" France	405,944	"
" Germany	7,823,042	"
Grand total	10,377,166	Gallo s

Over ten million gallons of the very cheapest, worst and most poisonous liquor that ever went down the throat of man! Oh, yes! Africa is being "opened up" with a vengeance! If the trading companies can only get a railroad built around the cataracts of the Congo, so as to get cheap liquor into the interior, we may confidently expect to see fifty million gallons flowing in annually, instead of only ten.

Now is it not high time that something should be done about it? Judge for yourself whether the question is a serious one; whether a great crime is not being committed under our very eyes; whether such a state of affairs in a savage country is not a shame and disgrace to civilization in general, and to Christianity in particular. Talk about the Dark Ages of the past! Why, the people of Africa are only just entering upon theirs—and it

is the gift of the nineteenth century, too! What
are education, progress and religion worth if they
cannot prevent the vultures of commerce from
preying upon the vitals of an ignorant and helpless race? At home, in our centers of enlightenment, a large proportion of us are so determined
to wreck our lives and fortunes by drink, and we
display so much devilish ingenuity in working out
our own ruin, despite all restraint, that the white
race seems destined to eternal drunkenness. But
with the savage races of Africa, the case is different. They are as plastic clay just now, and will
be whatever the stronger and more intelligent
forces of civilization make them. Shall we pour
out rum like water amongst them, and turn them
into degraded sots, worse than beasts, or shall we
resolutely demand that the rum sellers keep "hands
off"? Surely so great a cause as this—I cannot call
it a question, for there is but one side to it—demands the active support of even the most indifferent observer. Surely a higher object could not
be found than the rescue of Africa's dusky millions
from the horrors of intemperance.

CHAPTER VI.

FIXING THE RESPONSIBILITY.

The Congo Free-Rum State took its place definitely in the world no longer ago than year before last, and the present is only a faint foreshadowing of the future. With liquor pouring into Africa by the hundred thousand gallons, with bottles of rum and demijohns of gin in general use as currency, and 50 per cent. of what the natives produce paid for with liquor, what is to be the future of the Congo native? It is time for him to bow down to the unknown God and pray, " Save me from my friends!"

Do you ask who are the promoters of this gigantic evil, and the *particeps criminis* in the matter? The answer is easy. There are two sets of individuals implicated, and each is wholly to blame. Unless something is done at once to check this evil, there will be a third party to the crime, composed of the enlightened, high-principled men and women of Christendom who see this wholesale destruction of human souls, and yet are either too indifferent or too indolent, or both combined, to arouse and with a mighty effort put a quietus to this awful work.   At the imminent risk of being called a pessimist, an alarmist, a sensationalist, and finally a "crank," I propose to lay bare the evil, point to the ways and means by which it can be remedied, and lay the responsibility at the doors where it belongs.   When once this is done, woe unto the statesman and the citizen, the minister and the layman who turn a deaf ear to the cry from Macedonia.   Let those who legislate for the welfare of the nations, let those who seek to convert the world to Christianity, ignore this call, if they dare.

In fixing the responsibility for the state of affairs which exists to-day in West Africa, it is a question which should be named first,—the commercial miscreants who are doing the devil's work, or the statesmen composing the Berlin Conference who unanimously agreed to allow them to do it. On the whole, perhaps, the latter are entitled to precedence!

When the representatives of fourteen of the greatest and most enlightened Powers on the earth met at Berlin in 1884–5 to hold the great West African Conference, they settled definitely for the next twenty years, the political status of all the territory bordering on the Congo.   They held the Congo Free State in their hands, and shaped its

future to suit themselves. They said what it
should do, what it should not do, and what the
subjects of their sovereigns should be allowed to
do in it. And the Alpha and Omega of all their
deliberations was " trade," the " absolute freedom
of commerce," gain, national and individual advantage in hard cash. Did the members of that august assembly, which had Prince Bismarck for its
president, think of the naked savage in his grass
hut, and try to legislate for him? Four only out
of the fourteen did so, to the everlasting honor of
themselves and the countries they represented.
I will name them: The Hon. John A. Kasson,
representing the United States; Count de Launay,
for Italy; Sir Edward B. Malet, for Great Britain,
and Count Van der Straten, for Belgium. These
gentlemen pronounced strongly in favor of controlling the liquor traffic on the Congo and the
Niger. Let me give a brief compilation of the
deliberations on this point, extracted from Execu-
tive Document No. 247, 48th Congress, on the
" Congo Conference." The papers comprising
this document were laid before Congress by the
President in response to a resolution of the House
requesting copies of all official communications
regarding the Congo Conference.

The key-note of what should have been the deliberations of the Conference, and might have

been but for the accursed spirit of trade, was
sounded by Sir Edward Malet in the declaration
read by him at the first session, immediately following the opening speech of Prince Bismarck.
These were his words, and they deserve to be
branded with a red-hot iron upon the representatives of the rum-sellers who thwarted their purpose; the British Government has every reason to
be proud of her representation:

"I must, however, not lose sight of the fact
that in the opinion of the British Government, the
interests of commerce are not to be considered as
the exclusive subject of the deliberations of the
Conference.

"While it is desirable to secure a market in the
Congo country, the welfare of the natives is not
to be neglected.

"The natives, however, would lose more than
they would gain, if the freedom of commerce, being without any reasonable control, were allowed
to degenerate into license. I trust that precau-
tionary measures will be taken as regards legitimate
commerce, so that its introduction may, as far as
possible, secure the benefits of civilization to the
Africans, and the extinction of the evils which are
on a par with the slave trade in the interior,
whereby their progress is now retarded.

" I MUST REMEMBER THAT THE NATIVES ARE
NOT REPRESENTED AT THIS CONFERENCE, AND
THAT, NEVERTHELESS, THE DECISIONS OF THIS
BODY WILL BE OF THE GRAVEST IMPORTANCE
TO THEM.

" The principle which will secure the sympathy
and support of the Government of Her Britannic
Majesty, will be the promotion of legitimate commerce, with a guaranty of the equality of the
usage that shall be granted to all nations, *and of
the welfare of the natives.*"

There is a confession of faith! Would to
heaven that all the other members of the Conference had been similarly inspired. How different
would be the state of affairs to-day in the Dark
Continent!

In the second session of the Conference (November 19th) the Count de Launay declared in favor
of temperance in the following language, charac-
teristically diplomatic, it is true, but nevertheless
clear in meaning:

" To the liberty of commerce in general is at-
tached special questions, as those of the traffic in
arms and spirituous beverages. If the assembly
occupies itself with these questions, the plenipotentiary of the King [of Italy] will pronounce
himself in a manner conforming to the principles

of progress and civilization which form the constant rule of the Government of his Majesty."

During this same session our representative presented the views of his government in a formal address, but, unfortunately, his exact language in reference to the liquor traffic is not quoted. At the conclusion of the report of his address, however, the official protocol of the session (*e. g.*, the minutes) records the following statement:

" Mr. Kasson adds that he adheres to that part of Count de Launay's statement tending to control the introduction of liquors in the barbarous regions with which the Conference is occupied."

In the next letter to our Secretary of State, Mr. Kasson refers to the Count de Launay as follows: " In like manner I attract your attention to his suggestions touching the traffic in arms and spiritous liquors. I also, in the latter discussion in French, referred to the same subject, indicating the necessity of restraints on the liquor traffic with the natives, as shown by our experience in America."

In the third and fourth sessions of the Conference nothing was said concerning the liquor traffic, but at the latter, the plenipotentiary for Great Britain, whose government at that time was in absolute possession of the Lower Niger, proposed to the assembly an "Act of Navigation of the Niger," of which the following article formed a part:

"The transit of spirituous liquors is prohibited on the course of the Lower Niger.

"The Mussulman populations of the basins of the Central Niger and of Lake Chad, neither make nor drink alcoholic liquors. It would be disastrous if the well-being of these populations should be imperilled, even indirectly, by the introduction of the commerce of civilized countries.

"*If this article is accepted, the Government of Her Majesty engages to establish the regulations to put it in force.*"

The last paragraph is full of significance, and is very particularly commended to the notice of those who may feel inclined to say that it is impossible to prevent the importation of deadly liquors into West Africa. This article says distinctly, " I can protect the Niger people from the horrors of intemperance, and will do so, if you will let me; for I have voluntarily given you the right to decide this question with the rest."

Oh, England! It was a sad mistake when you left the decision of such a question to such a conference.

In its session of December 18, 1884, the Conference discussed the liquor question for the last time. The representatives of Great Britain, Italy, Bel-

gium, and the United States upheld the cause of
humanity, and declared in favor of controlling
the traffic in spirituous liquors. They were
strongly in favor of an act which should be calculated to reconcile the interests of commerce
with the inalienable rights of the African populations and the principles of humanity throughout
the whole extent of the territory of the Congo.

Then came the opposition. The representative of the Netherlands, M. Van der Hoeven,
held that they could not do more than to allow
the states established in Central Africa the right
to superintend the sale of liquors (*with no chance
to restrict the quantity*, be it understood).

The German representative, M. Busch, believed
that the control of the retail sale of drinks is at
present the only thing to do; but that measures of
this nature are not within the competence of the
Conference. (In other words, this Conference,
though clothed with supreme powers to make and
unmake, has not the power to frame a single law
touching the liquor traffic, except that it shall be
FREE!) M. Busch declares that he would not
dare to adhere to the proposition of Count Van
der Straten (to protect the negroes against the
abuse of strong drink), but he is ready at once to
join in a suggestion formulated by the commission.

The Baron de Courcel, for France, agreed with
M. Van der Hoeven that it is the control of the
retail sale of spirits which they should try to facil-
itate; but that is a matter of internal police which
belongs naturally to the local sovereignties.   M.
de Kusserow (also for Germany) like his colleague,
opposed restrictive enactments of all kinds, and
held that "it is in the initiative taken by the local
governments that will be found the best remedy
against the demoralization of the populations from
the abuse of strong drink."

Stripped of all ornamental verbiage, the naked
truth is as follows: The representatives of Holland, Germany, and France were totally opposed
to the enactment of any legislation aimed at *re-
stricting*, or even controlling the trade in liquor,
but they were most virtuously and generously
willing that the local governments in Africa
should be allowed to superintend the sale of liquors; that is to say, they were willing the local
authorities should say whether poisonous brandy
should be sold in quarts or pints, in flat bottles or
round ones!

What magnificent philanthropy! Such a waste-
ful flow of the milk of human kindness is enough
to make a wolf weep.

During this discussion, it is stated that Herr
Woerman declared that so far from being an evil,

the sale of spirituous liquors to the natives was of
great benefit to them, because it taught them the
value of trade, and brought them more effectually
under the influence of civilization!

The outcome of the whole discussion was this
" proposition respecting spirituous beverages"
entered " in protocol VI. by agreement," a sort
of belated P. P. S. to the postscript annexed to
the General Act. The reader cannot fail to notice the delicacy, nay, even tenderness, manifested
in the wording of this rare and rather sickly hot-
house production. Instead of being a distinct
declaration, it is a " proposition " (formerly a
" *suggestion*" *!*) and it is entered " by agreement"
instead of being *adopted*, fairly and squarely. In
the text, the Powers are so excessively modest and
retiring in their disposition, that they are afraid to
do more than insinuate; they "avow their wish,"
(at first it was " emit the desire"!) instead
of making an honest, front-faced, square-toed
declaration. But here is the " suggestion " or
" proposition " in full. It is an invertebrate of the
lowest order, having neither teeth, legs nor back-
bone.

"The Powers represented at the Conference, de-
siring that the indigenous population may be
guarded against the evils arising from the abuse
of strong drinks, avow their wish that an agree-

ment may be established between them to regulate
the difficulties which might arise on this subject,
in such a manner as to conciliate the rights of humanity with the interests of commerce, in so far as
these interests may be legitimate."

And this after it has already been agreed most
positively and beyond a peradventure that commerce and navigation shall be absolutely free,
excepting for pilotage and port-dues on vessels.
This "proposition" merely says: "I really wish I
could, but I can't. Be ye warmed and fed, but
keep hands off my precious commerce!" Of all
the subterfuges that were ever adopted to escape a
great responsibility, and throw dust in the eyes of
the world, it seems to me this is the most paltry and
inexcusable. On the part of some of the plenipotentiaries there was too much courtesy, and not enough
firmness; while on the part of the remainder there
was a conspicuous lack of honesty and humanity, joined to inordinate selfishness and greed.   If
ever a set of men failed in the discharge of their
duty, were false to their trust and deliberately fostered a gigantic evil, it was those members of the
Berlin Conference who insisted upon free trade
in rum on the Congo.   It is a sickening sight to
see great nations like Germany and France, so
fiercely vigilant in shielding their own subjects
against all harm from without, pander to the

demands of their rum-exporters for the privilege
of debasing the blacks past all hope of rescue.

O Commerce! How .many crimes are committed in thy name! Trade is the new Moloch on
whose altar millions of victims are sacrificed annually. It was even Christian England that
opened with her bayonets the seaports of China
for the sale of the opium which her Anglo-Indian
planters produced. When "trade" demands fresh
victims they must be produced, even though it re-
quires the hand of a statesman or a sovereign to
lead them forth. So long as statesmen bow
meekly before the power which is wielded by the
promoters of vice, just so long will vice be pro-
moted and the devil's harvest be reaped day by
day.

Just so long as rum may be sold in Africa without let or hindrance, by whomsoever can send it
there, just so long will there be unprincipled merchants to ship it and retail it among the natives.
If the natives had happened to prefer opium or
arsenic, why, then, opium and arsenic would now
be used as currency instead of gin. Every country
has a grand army of unhanged liquor-sellers, any
one of whom, for the sake of "business" and a
profit of three cents, will sell a glass of liquor
with the knowledge that it will send its purchaser
into the gutter the next moment.

All men who are mean enough to promote vice
for money deserve to be hanged, or else put where
they can prey only upon each other. It is bad
enough for one educated European to sell intoxicants to another; but what shall we say of the
intelligent white man who sows drunkenness, disease, degradation and death broadcast among the
ignorant blacks, who, like so many children in
knowledge are just emerging from savagery.
Since these murderers of morals are without conscience, their depredations should be limited by
law, even if all the rest of this great world has
not the power to suppress them entirely.

When we come to sum up our evidence, and fix
the responsibility for the condition of Africa upon
the shoulders to which it belongs, there is no difficulty about pointing out the offenders.

First of all come those members of the Congo
Conference who resisted all efforts to provide protection for the morals of the natives.   Unfortunately, the Conference was so constituted that no
measure could be adopted without a unanimous
vote of the whole fourteen plenipotentiaries, so
we were treated to the unique spectacle of a delib-
erative assembly in which the minority ruled.

Next come the great legislative bodies of the
various powers who permit their merchants and
chartered trading companies to ship vast quantities

of intoxicating liquors to their respective possessions in Africa. For example, England is to blame
for permitting the sale of spirits to natives in any
British Colony, and especially in Africa. And
again, the various Colonial governments of the
African colonies are to be held directly accountable for not only permitting but authorizing, by
legal enactment, the sale of spirits amongst the
natives, regardless of quantity or quality. The
Parliaments of Cape Colony and Natal are directly
responsible for the work of degradation and extermination that is going on amongst the Korannas,
and for such criminal indifference on the part of
South Africa there is neither palliation nor excuse.
In resolutely permitting the infernal traffic in
spirits to go on they are, both individually and col-
lectively, guilty of a high crime; and if ever criminal carelessness deserves a place behind prison-
bars, it deserves it in Cape Colony.

Every colony has its code of laws, whether
made in the governing body at home or in
its own Colonial government; so there need be
no trouble whatever in laying the blame for free
rum at the right door. Whoever enacts the laws
for a colony is bound by the highest obligations to
protect the morals of the indigenous races within
its borders from all the vices of civilization, and
especially from the curse of civilized liquor.

Whoever has the power to protect a savage race, and fails to exercise it to its uttermost limit, entails upon himself a fearful responsibility; and for the mischief that is done under his hand and seal he must be held accountable. It may be impossible to enforce strict prohibition laws in this country or in England, where a meteor cannot fall without striking a saloon or a distillery; but in an African colony the case is very different. *In all those countries, strict temperance can easily be enforced.* It can be done by prohibiting the importation of liquors, and also prohibiting their sale. White men are few, and the doings of each one are known, so that it is a very difficult, nay, impossible matter, to evade a temperance law, *provided the government really determines to enforce it.*

The churches are to blame for not seeing the necessity for striking at the root of such a gigantic evil, and for not striking at it with all their strength. It is amazing that such short-sightedness could have prevailed for so long a time. Can there be any question about the matter? Let us take up a convenient case and see, for the benefit of those who believe that the missionaries are spending their efforts to the best advantage, for the greatest good to the greatest number.

Let us take South Africa as the best possible illustration, from both points of view. For many

years this has been the very garden-spot of the
churches for foreign missionary work. The
ground has been hallowed by the tread of such
missionaries as Dr. Livingstone, Dr. Moffatt, the
Coillard family, and a host of others of all denominations. There has been, comparatively
speaking, no lack of laborers in the field, nor lack
of zeal. Well, "what of the night?"

The Korannas and Hottentots of Cape Colony
and Griqualand, instead of being lifted higher by the
missionaries, are actually being exterminated by
the spirits of the English traders. Let me quote
Dr. Holub again:

"Lazy and dirty, crafty and generally untruth-
ful, * * * capable of well-nigh any crime for the
sake of fire-water—to my mind, they [the Kor-
annas] offer an example of humanity as degraded
and loathsome as can be imagined. Employ them
in the far wilderness, *where no European is at
hand to supply them with spirits,* and it is possible
they might be more desirable than Kaffres, * * but
after making several trials of them myself, and
using every effort to *keep them sober,* I was always
compelled to give up in despair.

"It is only when he is without the means of procuring brandy, which is his sole and engrossing
desire, that a Koranna is ever known to rouse himself from his habitual sloth. * * * *As a distinct*

race, the Korannas are dying out.   In this respect,
they are sharing the lot of the Hottentots proper,
who dwell in Cape Colony and Griqualand.   So
continual has been the diminution of their number
that they are not half what they formerly were,
and their possessions have diminished in a still
greater proportion."

And this in spite of the missionaries.   Now can
this condition of things be explained away?
Hardly.   What are a thousand individual converts
to the wiping out of two whole tribes by the vices
of civilization?   How different might have been
the result, had the churches and missionaries made
an assault in force on the Cape Parliament, and
besieged that honorable body until it enacted pro-
hibitory laws!   But no, a few leaves were doctored,
and the whole trunk was left to wither.   *Shall we
see the same disastrous experiment repeated in the
Congo Free State?*

CHAPTER VII.

"THOU ART THY BROTHER'S KEEPER."

Reader, suppose it should come to your knowledge that several of the largest publishing houses in New York City were publishing and introducing among the millions of school children in the United States, millions of dime novels of the most virulent type, all infected with small-pox, scarlet fever and diphtheria. Suppose that this awful slaughter of the innocents was going on with the sanction of the city of New York, of the State Legislature, and of Congress itself, and was backed by millions of money, as well as a powerful lobby. What would you do about it? Would you merely be shocked by the disclosure, call it no affair of yours, and put the whole disagreeable subject as far from you as possible? I think not. You would shut your teeth together, and prepare for war. You would attack all parties who were responsible for such a state of affairs. You would make it your special business to begin a mighty crusade against the evil, and so far from allowing it to go by default as "nobody's business," you would make it your very particular business, and follow it up on that basis. If you should chance to be another Ralph Nickleby, or Squeers, or Daniel Quilp, or Murdstone, or Gabriel Grubb, of course you would say it was no affair of yours; and if the children want to be such fools, it is not your business to hinder them.

Now, this hypothetical case is an exact parallel of what the liquor traders are doing with liquor among the savages of Africa this day, in the year of our Lord eighteen hundred and eighty-seven. The people there are merely grown-up children, nothing more, with no more sense of the deadly hurtfulness of the vices of civilization than have the gorillas of the forest. They are bad enough as they are, heaven knows, so ignorant and vicious naturally, that Monteiro despairs of their future, even with liquor left out of it. Since they are naturally so prone to evil, so ignorant and so vicious, what will they become with the addition of universal drunkenness!

Reader, this matter demands your attention, your interest and your personal influence in the cause of humanity. Every enlightened man and woman in the whole Christian world shares the responsibility for the curse of Africa from the moment he or she is made aware of the crime. A fearful burden of responsibility rests upon the in-

telligent portion of the European race, and every
day its bulk is rising higher and higher. "Thou
art thy brother's keeper," and therefore it is your
business and mine to do our utmost toward protecting the savage races of Africa—and the whole
world for that matter—from the serpent which is
more deadly than the serpent of the Nile, the
worm of the still. You cannot shift your share of
the responsibility to the shoulders of any one else;
you must work it off, or there it will remain.

Shall we, who boast so proudly of our education, intelligence and progress; of our religion,
philanthropy, our mental and moral culture; in
short, our civilization,—shall we sit calmly down,
cloaked with egotism and self-righteousness, and
see our boasted civilization plant its vices un-
checked and unrebuked among simple savages,
and slay them in millions? Answer me, yes or
no. Do not equivocate, do not look about for a
loophole by which to escape, but *answer*, honestly,
as you hope to live. In doing so, remember that
he who countenances a crime shares the guilt of
the chief criminal.

It will not suffice to say that the evil has gone
so far that it is too late to do anything, or that the
power of the African trading companies is too
great to overcome; or that governments cannot be
influenced; or that a private individual can do

nothing; for none of these things are true. There are enough honest men and women in the world, and enough editors and statesmen, who do not fear the liquor interest, to cause every port in Africa to be hermetically sealed against spirituous liquors in two years' time, if they would but do what lies in their power to accomplish that end. I am well convinced that it is not only possible, but clearly *practicable* to stop the importation of liquor into Africa for sale among the natives. I consider it a perfectly feasible undertaking, and one which could surely be accomplished by a general effort on the part of those who have a duty in the matter. With a goodly array of workers and an adequate campaign fund, success would be certain, barring such misfortunes as stupid generalship.

We come now to consider ways and means. At this point I reluctantly take leave of truths so apparent as to be unanswerable, and enter the field of personal opinion.

Having studied the problem with some attention, I may at least be pardoned for giving some of my conclusions.

In the first place, the end sought can only be gained by a forward movement along the whole line, and an assault in force, led by the ablest generals in the field. To start with, it will be necessary to enlist the sympathy and active support of

the press everywhere. The newspapers, maga-
zines and reviews of all sorts, secular, religious,
literary, scientific and what-not—must constitute
the heavy artillery of the fight, whose thunders
will tell the news of the battle in even the remot-
est corners of the earth. Editors must be appealed
to, articles must be written, meetings must be held
and reported; and, in short, every effort must be
made to interest the public in the matter, and enlist active support in all quarters.

Churches of all denominations should make the
struggle a personal matter, and every minister of
the gospel should agitate the question to the very
uttermost, in season and out of season, until success is attained. Sermons should be preached on
the subject again and again, and such special efforts made as would seem calculated to further the
desired end.

The temperance and foreign missionary societies in particular should concentrate their efforts in
the direction of *no rum in Africa*, and all foreign
mission work of a general nature should be held
of secondary importance until the end sought is
obtained. The Congo missionaries should fight
free rum just now, instead of translating the Bible
for savages who have no written language, and
teaching theology to a handful of blacks here and
there. Time enough for doctrinal teaching and

Biblical translations when Free Rum is laid in its grave.

The Woman's Christian Temperance Union has already taken the initiative in bringing this matter to the attention of the public in general, and Congress in particular. Its machinery is already in motion for work of this character, and its influence will soon be felt around the world. In the distribution of printed matter, the circulation of petitions, and all such work, this great organization may well be expected to take the lead.

At the earliest possible moment, Congress must be appealed to in distinct terms, to pass an act inviting the other great powers of the original fourteen to join the United States in an effort to remedy this monstrous abuse, which has grown out of too free trade on the Congo. Owing to the manner in which the Congo Free State came into political existence, the liquor traffic there cannot be reached without the consent of the powers. This might be obtained by diplomatic correspondence, but it is almost certain that if reliance is placed on that method of procedure, it would result in nothing whatever. There would be documents upon documents exchanged, "officially," long delays between questions and answers, and the question would drag itself by correspondence through the remainder of this century without any definite end being attained. Diplomacy moves slowly enough, even at best, when the diplomats are face to face. While it might be possible to secure the concurrence of all the powers in some effective, restrictive measure, another conference of plenipotentiaries is what is needed. It is the duty of the United States Government, 1. To call the attention of the other powers to the monstrous abuse of the liquor traffic, and in so forcible a manner as to command attention; 2. To propose a conference of delegates to be held in the city of Washington; 3. To formally issue invitations to the powers, and 4. To champion the cause of temperance throughout Africa. To whom shall we look for a champion if not to the government of the most intelligent and humane people on the face of the earth?

It is idle for any one to say that the difficulties in the way are too many, too great, and that the thing cannot be done. An American should be ashamed to say so. Is our ingenuity so feeble, are we so barren of resources, so impoverished for the sinews of war, so weak-spirited and impotent that we must turn and fly affrighted by the terrible front of our adversary, before a blow is struck on either side? For shame! Why, if there were only a few millions of money to be made by enforcing temperance in Africa, there would be ten thousand capitalists clamoring at the doors of Congress to-morrow for the exclusive privilege of performing the task. What is more, every company bidding for the privilege, would be ready to deposit ten million dollars as a guaranty of success, to be forfeited in case of failure. If the Mighty Dollar was only there, there would be no need to raise a temperance army by conscription; we should be overwhelmed with volunteers.

Just how the quietus should be placed on free rum, is also a matter of opinion.

It will be no child's play to enact laws for the suppression of the liquor traffic on the Congo, and enforce them. If any permanent good is to be accomplished there must be no temporizing, no making of terms with the devil, nor half-way measures of any kind. Any laws for the " regulation " of the traffic are sure to be evaded. Nothing short of absolute and unconditional suppression of the importation of intoxicants will ever reach the root of the evil. " But," the trader will cry out, " that cannot be done without granting the local authorities the right to search all vessels." Very well, then let them be searched, from stem to stern, from deck to keelson, and whenever liquors are found pour them into the Congo instantly. " It will cripple commerce," whines the trader again, " and prevent the development of the coun-

try." We reply, commerce that can live and
thrive only by the promotion of vice amongst an
aboriginal race deserves to be strangled in its cradle.
As matters stand at present, the " development of .
Africa " of which we hear so much, when stripped
of its false colors, means simply the enrichment of
a few European traders and manufacturers at the
cost of the moral degradation of fifty million natives. Not even the slave-trade has ever done so
much harm to the Congo blacks as intemperance
bids fair to do, and that right speedily.

It seems clear that the two things to be done by
way of beginning are, (1) to secure in this
country and the various countries of Europe the
legislation necessary to positively prohibit the .ex-
portation of intoxicating liquors to Africa, or to
any other part of the globe for transshipment
thither, and (2) also the legislation in Europe and
in the colonies of Africa necessary to hermetically
seal every port and coast-line against the importation of intoxicating liquors. Let spirits be declared contraband, subject to immediate confiscation
wherever and whenever found in Africa, whether
ashore or afloat, and subject the owner thereof to
a heavy fine, and you will see the rivers of rum
stop short, never to go again, so long as the guardians of the people do their duty. In such an
act as the above might be included a law against

the manufacture of spirits in Africa, and against
the possession of appliances for manufacture.

The thing is perfectly feasible. When Sir
Edward Malet proposed that the traffic in spirituous
liquors should be prohibited on the Congo, he
declared most pointedly that " if this article is accepted, the government of Her Majesty engages to
establish the regulations to put it in force." So
much for the Queen's ability to rule her portion
of Africa. Are the governments of France, Germany, the Netherlands, Belgium, Spain and
Portugal less able to enforce good laws in their
colonies? By no means.

In any movement looking to the enforcement of
temperance in Africa, and the amelioration of the
condition of the people, the government of the
United States could count to a certainty on the
hearty co-operation of England, Belgium, and
Italy, and probably France also. Austria, Spain,
Russia, Portugal, Turkey, Sweden, Norway
and Denmark would be unopposed to the movement, and without doubt could easily be persuaded
to enlist in the cause of humanity. The trouble
would come with Germany and the Netherlands.
The colonial trade bee is buzzing furiously in the
Dutch and German bonnet. In Germany, especially, the interest in Bismarck's Colonial policy is
now rampant, and the monied interests at stake

will struggle hard to retain all the privileges they
now enjoy.   The Woermans of both Germany
and Holland will marshal all their forces, appeal
to their governments, and spend money without
stint to protect the precious privilege they now
enjoy of getting rich by making negroes drunk.
The trading companies will all fight to the death
for free rum everywhere in Africa, and the fortunes they have at stake will make them fight
with the energy of fear and despair.

Germany and Holland will be the battle-ground
for the great struggle.   In case those two governments are obstinate to the last in maintaining their
present position, shall they be allowed to dictate
the policy of the other twelve powers in a matter
which involves the moral and material welfare of
so many millions?   No, a thousand times no. But
then it cannot be possible that the statesmen of
those two countries are so devoid of all feelings
of humanity as to refuse to co-operate in such a
movement.

When the time comes to influence great legislative bodies, rulers with crowned heads, and rulers
without, every one who is willing to lend a helping
hand can render valuable aid.   Monster petitions
are good things, sometimes, though not often, and
in such cases as the present, I consider direct personal appeals to Cabinet Ministers, or Congressmen,

or Members of Parliament, or delegates of much
greater power. If you know a legislator, appeal
to him, and ask his attention to the matter as a personal favor. If you do not know a congressman,
then seek the acquaintance of some for this special
purpose. In such a cause, one has a right to ask
for a vote, to exact a promise, to demand assistance
of all kinds from any one who can render any.
Write letters to your friends, and in the name of
friendship demand their aid. Wherever it is
thought a formal petition with signatures would
be effective, draw one up and circulate it vigor-
ously. If money is needed for campaign documents, *take up a collection.*

If the movement suggested is ever started it
should never, under any circumstances, be merged
or confounded with any other temperance movement whatsoever. This is a *special case*, and can
be made to command attention when any other
temperance question would fall on deaf ears. In
this, it is necessary to work for certain specific
things, and keep the main object from being ob-
scured by side issues. By doing this, it will be
possible to enlist active support and warm sympathy in quarters whence none would come for
any other effort of a less urgent kind. Do not
ask for impossible things, but set the mark aright
and go straight at it every time.

Something must be done at once, if ever, to
stop the flow of intoxicants into Africa and among
the natives. It is a Herculean task, but if the political forces which brought the Congo Free State
into existence, combined with those of the Church
and the advocates of temperance, are not sufficient
to put a quietus upon this rum traffic, then let
Europe and America acknowledge with shame
that rum is king. If the Church has more missionaries, let some of them be sent to Herr Woerman and others of his kind in Germany and
Holland, England or America, or wherever they
are to be found. Save the black man from his
friends,—those who would make his country free
and accessible at all points to the boats and caravans of the gin peddler.

From all accounts, no aborigines have ever
shown such a universal passion for strong drink
as possesses these people. If liquor can be kept
away from them, there is room for hope that the
missionaries can bring them into the light, and
make civilization a blessing to them instead of a
curse. Who are the most powerful, the traders
who desire to get rich out of palm oil and India-
rubber purchased with gin, or the fourteen Christian nations participating in the Conference, with
their 388,000,000 of Christians? America has 65
foreign missionary societies, England 71, and the

Continent 57, exclusive of those of the Roman
Catholic Church.   Are they powerful enough to
cope with the rum traffic on the Congo?   Herr
Woerman and his colleagues have cut out work
for them, and it will require all the combined influence they can muster to persuade Germany and
Holland to allow the rest of the Christian world
to enforce temperance on the Congo.   The rights
of the money-makers are so sacred, you know.

Will the Boards of Foreign Missions try to save
the tree by doctoring its leaves, one by one, while
the sap is being poisoned in the roots?   We will
see.

CHAPTER VIII.

The People to be Protected.

I wish I could truthfully say that the inhabitants of the great Congo basin are a fine race of people; but I cannot. It would be much more pleasant if the savages, in whom we are called upon to interest ourselves, could be described as being intelligent, amiable and teachable, like the Polynesians generally; or of high moral and social character, like the Dyaks; or hospitable to the last degree, like the Eskimo; or even as brave and enterprising in war as the Kaffirs of the South. It is much more satisfactory to work for a really noble savage with some redeeming qualities than for one who has many of the bad qualities a man should not have, and comparatively few of the redeeming features. But the truth is the truth, and it must be told. The Congo natives are about as bad savages as nature has any business to produce. To be sure, they are not so low and brutelike as the Bushmen or the native Australians, nor so ignorant as the Veddahs, nor so murderously cruel as the Dahomans, or even some of our noble redskins, for that matter. Their depravity and ignorance is not so bad as to be without a parallel, but, like Mercutio's wound, "it is enough." If any Christian Hercules seeks an Augean stable to cleanse, one of the very rankest kind, behold it in Africa. To those who believe in the ultimate conversion of the world, who believe in the millennium,—a hundred million dusky hands beckon from the swampy jungles and burning plains of the Dark Continent, saying more plainly than words, "Come over into Macedonia and help us."

Before going farther, let me place before the reader Mr. Stanley's figures representing " the state of our actual knowledge of the population of the Congo basin :"*

SECTION.	Area in Sq. Miles	Population per Sq. Mi.	Number of Population
Lower Congo.................	33,000	about 9	297,000
Upper Congo	1,090,000	" 40	43,884,000
Lualaba.........................	246,000	" 20	4,920,000
Chambezi, with Bangweblo.....	46,000	" 10	460,000
Tanganyika	93,000	" 25	2,325,000
	1,508,000	average 34	51,886,000

The above estimate is of the actual geographical basin of the Congo and all its tributaries, up to the western shore of Lake Tanganyika. In order to show, however, just how this vast population is divided politically, it is necessary to reproduce Mr. Stanley's other table of area and population:

*"The Congo" Vol. I. page 364.

THE CONGO BASIN.	Divisional Areas Sq Miles	Population
French Territory.................	64,400	2,121,600
Po tuguese Territory............	30,700	276,300
Unclaimed	349,700	6,910,000
Free State of the Congo.........	1,065,200	42,608,000
	1,508,000	51,886,000

In order to obtain a sharply defined bird's-eye view of the Congo native and his country, we must take them up feature by feature and call to our aid the observations of all available authorities.

The first thing, then, to be considered is

THE COUNTRY.

Surface.—Along the coast and for one hundred miles back, the country is low, level, swampy, miasmatic and pestilential, but very rich. Above that to Stanley Pool and beyond, the country is one vast region of sand and clay hills, covered with thick jungle, poor and unproductive, as a rule, although there are here and there fertile spots, usually in close proximity to villages. The river valleys are also very fertile, but not cultivated. Excepting the Masamba forest, which is of small extent, there is no heavily timbered country between Ponta de Lenna and Stanley Pool, and even along the banks of the Congo there are only a few trees of any considerable size. The forest growth is low, scrubby, and not fit for lumber; neither is there any stone fit for building purposes save in the bed of the great river, and at a few points along its banks. No coal has yet been discovered, nor any other mineral or metal in the Congo valley which can be considered as adding materially to the wealth of the country. In short, between Stanley Pool and the fertile Coast Country, the land is a barren wilderness of sand and clay hills, unproductive, inhospitable, and of precious little value to anybody. The only roads in the country are the narrow paths from village to village, so narrow that all marching must be done in Indian file. "In the valleys, one must march many miles through the tall, rank grass, often twelve to twenty feet high, without being able to see out either right, left or overhead.

"It not unfrequently happens that the coast caravans and Houssas couriers take the wrong path and travel many miles, and even days out of their way, before finding their mistake." (*Tisdel*).

Above Stanley Pool, the tropical luxuriance and richness of soil begin. The country is fertile and rich in natural products, the forests are heavy, and the population per square mile is more than four times as great as on the Lower Congo. Only one difficulty stands in the way of the "development" of this region, but that is of colossal dimensions. The cataracts of the Congo oblige

commerce to travel by land, and the absence of
all vehicles and beasts of burden, excepting men,
makes the cost of transportation so great as to almost prohibit it altogether.   But then, the natural
riches are there, and the commercial world will
either find a way to them or *make* one.

Climate.—Throughout the whole of the Lower
Congo country, the climate is very deadly.   Indeed, there is probably nowhere else on the face
of the earth so great an extent of territory which is
everywhere so fatal in its effects on civilized men.
Thus far, the mortality among the white men who
have undertaken to live on the Lower Congo has
been something fearful to think of.   Of the six
hundred or more white men who have engaged
with the African International Association to
serve it three years, only five have been able to
remain the full contract time (Tisdel).   It is considered that in general, a continuous residence of
eighteen months is all a white man can stand.
Mr. Tisdel declares in an official communication
to the Secretary of State, that nine-tenths of the
missionaries who have gone to the Lower Congo
have died from the effects of the climate!   The
natives, of course, are able to withstand all the
evils the climate can bring against them, but it
must be admitted that intense heat, miasmatic ex-
halations, malignant mists from deadly swamps,

scanty food, and unwholesome water do not constitute an "environment" calculated to promote
the moral or intellectual progress of any savage.
Surrounded as he is by such conditions, it is really
surprising that the natives of the Lower Congo
and the Coast Country are as far from the lowest
round of the social ladder as they really are.

Above Stanley Pool, or, in other words, on the
Upper Congo, the climate is much better every
way. Where the vegetation is the most luxuriant,
as at the Equator Station, for example, the Europeans are the healthiest. Naturally, the Upper
Congo country is the garden spot of Africa, and
in spite of the present hostility of some of the natives at a few points, the chances are, that if *ju-
diciously* "developed," it will eventually produce
the finest types of the African race, as well as the
greatest commercial riches. If *rum* can be kept
from these people, and white thieves, liars and
libertines excluded also; if they can be shown
what a multitude of blessings flow from peace,
sobriety, honesty and industry, their future progress upward is assured.

Productions.—The commercial products of the
Congo basin are India-rubber, palm oil, palm nuts,
ground nuts, gum copal, camwood, wax, ivory,
orchilla weed, cola nuts, baobab fibre, gum traga-
canth, myrrh, nutmeg, ginger, frankincense, coffee,

castor seed, rattan canes, bark cloth, castor-oil nuts, copper, feathers, skins and hides. It will be noticed that this list includes not even one staple food product save the ground-nut. Horses and cattle are unknown, and the fact that the country produces no suitable food for these invaluable beasts of burden retards its development to an incalculable extent.

The native food products of the country (the great majority of which must be considered as belonging to the Upper Congo) are ground-nuts, bananas, plantains, manioc or cassava, maize, sugar-cane, millet, yams, sweet potatoes, beans, brinjalls, cucumbers, melons, pumpkins, tomatoes, etc. From Stanley Pool eastward, the officers of the International Association have introduced mangoes, papaws, oranges, limes, coffee, pineapples, guavas, cabbages, Irish potatoes, and onions, all of which appear to thrive.

THE PEOPLE.

Tribal Divisions.—To the casual observer, tribal distinctions in the Congo basin are by no means sharply defined. To judge by Mr. Stanley's records, one could hardly throw a brick-bat anywhere along the Congo without hitting a king or an independent chief. Between the two, the line of demarkation is very faintly drawn, and it is hard to say where the independent chief leaves off, and where the king begins. Between Banana Point and Stanley Falls, a distance of 1,413 miles, Mr. Stanley and his officers made over 450 treaties with native rulers, or one for about every three miles, on an average of the whole distance.

Government.—Kingships are hereditary and usually descend to a nephew. The great tribes are broken up into innumerable independent communities and villages, over which the village or district chiefs hold a sway which is more nominal than actual. If the chief's conduct fails to satisfy his constituents, he is liable to be deposed on short notice unless the office is hereditary. Each tribe is generally hostile to all its neighbors, and although wars are frequent, pitched battles of a sanguinary nature are rare. No standing armies are maintained, but, as is fast becoming the case in some of the continental monarchies, in times of war the entire male population constitutes the army.

The classes in society are four: king and royal family, chiefs, common people and slaves. The village chief and his family constitute the legislative and judicial council, from which it is lawful to appeal to the king, in case a king is acknowledged. A king, of course, maintains a council of ministers, which constitutes the highest court. Trials by or-

deal are universal, that by drinking a poison called
"cassia" being most common. If the poison acts
as an emetic, the accursed is declared innocent;
but if it acts as a purgative,—and it is certain to do
one or the other,—he is considered guilty beyond
a doubt, and is killed forthwith. An accused
person may drink the poison by proxy, *e. g.*, by a
slave, and stake his chances on the result.

Physique.—In physical characters, very great
differences are observed, so much so that it is impossible to describe a type common to all. There
is no special physiognomy. Even the thick lips
and flat nose are by no means universal. Strong
tendencies toward the Arab type are often observ-
able, due, without doubt, to an infusion of Arab
blood. The people are generally of middle stature,
and compare in general physique very favorably
with the best types of the African race. Judged by
their physiognomy, they must be considered perfectly capable of a high degree of development,
both mentally and morally.

The Family.—The practice of polygamy is
universal, and by the women is considered highly
desirable. As elsewhere, the number of wives a
man may have depends upon his wealth. A
widow belongs to the eldest surviving brother of
the deceased. A princess can choose her own husband from beneath her own rank if she desires,

and she has absolute power over him, even to taking his life. The marriage ceremony consists in
each of the contracting parties cooking a fowl for
the other. Children are always desired, and in-
fanticide is almost unknown. Family affection is
quite strong,—a most hopeful feature in any savage. It is customary, however, for daughters to
be sold to the wealthy.

Morals.—Chief among the few virtues of the
Congo native stands hospitality to each other.
But that cannot be counted upon for strangers.
Travelers agree in reporting that to strangers the
men are only sometimes hospitable, but the women
are always so., But even to this rule, we must note
an exception, viz., at Kouamout Station, on the
Upper Congo. Mr. Tisdel declares that when he
left this station, preparations were being made to
withdraw from it, "on account of the thieving pro-
pensities and hostilities of the women, who are the
governing power in the tribes of the Kouamout,
the men having no voice whatever." As before
remarked, family affection is strong, and politeness
prevails in social intercourse. There is a universal
dislike to being considered niggardly, and a general desire to be praised for generosity. In their
dealings with each other, the people have the rep-
utation of being honest and truthful, but in general
Mr. Tisdel declares them (of the Lower Congo at

least) to be "a cruel, treacherous, thieving set."
The Lower Congo people are very indolent, passionately fond of liquor and drunkenness, and
although among the *married*, unfaithfulness is
considered a great crime if the wife is guilty of it
without the husband's knowledge, yet various
immoral practices are indulged in, especially
among the unmarried.

The Congo people are extremely dirty, even
filthy in their mode of life, and especially in the
preparation of their food, and but little sense of
decency is manifested by the females. One traveler declares that "kings and fetish priests of the
Lower Congo make laws or rules which are of
the most cruel character, and the sacrifice of human life is as common within the Congo Valley as
it is in the kingdoms of Dahomey or Ashantee."
But this report is altogether too sanguinary. All
along the Congo, and to a great extent along the
coast also, it is a common thing to sacrifice slaves
on certain occasions. At Equator Station, the
Europeans in charge once witnessed the murder—
by beheading—which they were quite powerless
to prevent, of fourteen slaves, who were killed
that they might accompany the departed spirit of
an old chief. The African is nothing if not cruel,
and for him might always makes right.

The morals of the Coast negroes are shockingly

depraved, and it is an undeniable fact that the natives nearest the haunts of civilization are morally
the lowest and most depraved.   For instance, let
me quote this from Mr. Spencer's "Descriptive
Sociology." [The Coast negroes are] "addicted
to drunkenness, especially after intercourse with
Europeans. * * * The greatest dishonesty
prevails where the longest and most extensive intercourse has been had with Europeans."

And from Laird and Oldfield (Vol. I., p. 107),
"A people so thoroughly debased, demoralized, degraded," as the natives of the Delta of the Niger,
"I could not have conceived existed within a few
miles of ports which British ships have frequented
for a century.   But it only adds another to former
proofs that the intercourse between civilized and
savage nations has hitherto been productive of
anything but good to the latter."

It is universally conceded that the moral sentiments of the negroes of the far interior, who have
never felt the influence of civilization even in the
slightest degree, are far superior to those of the
negroes nearer the coast, who have felt the effect
of European and American commerce.

Education.—Of this, the Congo people have
none. They have no written language, nor even
picture writings, nor even unwritten literature.
They have no folk-lore to speak of, and few tra-

ditions save those known only by the fetish priests.
The people are not only densely ignorant but vicious. But let us divide the subject a little and consider, first, the people of the Lower Congo, or
below Stanley Pool.

The latest authority is Mr. N. P. Tisdel, special
agent of our Department of State.   The following is from his official report, as it appears in Consular Reports, No. 55:

Ignorance and Immorality of the Tribes.—"Education in any sense of the word is wholly unknown.   The natives live like brutes, and seem to
have no idea above the brute creation.   There are
occasional exceptions to this rule, where in the up
country you may find here and there, persons
showing signs of intelligence far above the ordinary.   They even may, and do, make good
rules for the government of their market places,
and some of them display great shrewdness in
barter and trade ; yet it is an indisputable fact
that the people are without the first rudiments
of an education, and efforts which have been made
to instruct them have proven failures.

"As to the general intelligence of the people, I
could observe very little difference between them.
They are, however, a shrewd, cunning, though
thoroughly unprincipled people. The tribes around
and above Stanley Pool are perhaps superior to

those of the low-land; certainly they surpass the
people of the low country in treachery and cruelty;
and I doubt whether anything can ever be done to
inspire them with a wish, even, to become educated.
They do not know what it means.   Their mode
of life and their every-day surroundings cannot be
changed.   The population is too great, and as they
live now, so they have lived for ages past.   Their
morals are of the lowest type.   They have no regard whatever for virtue, and their immoral practices place them quite as low in this respect as are
the apes and monkeys of the low countries."

This is the view of an honest pessimist who has
seen the Congo native at home.   Apparently, Mr.
Tisdel despairs of the black man's future.   But
even the great optimist, Mr. Stanley, has declared
that the people of the Congo basin are "ferocious
savages, devoted to abominable cannibalism and
the wanton murder of inoffensive people, friendly
when it is clearly to their interest to be so, but
suspicious and revengeful, arrogant at times, and
dangerous when under the influence of liquor,
lazy and fond of gin."   Of the Lower Congo
people, however, Mr. Stanley also declares they
are teachable and amenable to improvement and
discipline, but Mr. Tisdel informs us in the report
already alluded to that, "as a rule, these people are
a cruel, treacherous, thieving set, and, notwithstand-

ing published reports to the contrary, it is not safe
for a white man to travel without an armed escort."
It must be borne in mind, however, that by fair
dealing the officers of the Congo Free State, or
rather of the International African Association,
have made peace all along the river, save at Falls
Station and Aruwimi, which have been abandoned
because of the repeated attacks made upon them
by the Arab traders, and at Bolobo and Kouamout
Stations, which the hostilities of the natives have
also made untenable.

The natives of the Upper Congo, Mr. Stanley
declares in various parts of his last work, are more
amiable, more intelligent, skillful and industrious
than those on the lower river, and along the coast.
Of their drinking habits (*i. e.*, of the Inland
negroes generally) it is asserted that except where
they have not had much intercourse with the whites,
the negroes cannot be accused of being specially
addicted to intoxicating liquors. (*Waitz, Vol. I.,
p. 86.*)

The question of educating, or rather, let us say,
of improving the native, is a most serious one.

According to Mr. Monteiro (p. 136) the intellectual prospects of the negro are as dark as his
own skin; and, sad to say, Mr. Dennett, the latest
authority, holds the same discouraging opinion.
Says the former: "To sum up the negro character,

it is·deficient in the passions and in their corre-
sponding virtues, and the life of the negro in his
primitive condition, apparently so peaceful and
innocent (?) is not that of an unsophisticated state
of existence, but is due to what may be described
as an organically rudimentary form of mind, and
consequently capable of but little development to
a higher type; mere peaceable, vegetarian, prolific
human rabbits and guinea pigs, in fact; they may
be tamed and taught to read, write, sing psalms,
and other tricks, but negroes they must remain to
the end of the chapter."

Such sentiments as the above are hopelessly
pessimistic as regards the future of the Africans,
but they serve well to show the very primitive
condition of the people. They show how sadly
they need protection from vices of which they know
not the effects, and which we know, only too well,
would render their condition by far more hopeless
than it is. With sober natives, the educator can
do *something*, but with natives passionately fond
of drunkenness, nothing whatever. The people
of Africa *can* be taught the value of peace, honesty
and industry, and when they have learned these les-
sons thoroughly, it will *then* be time enough to
see whether their minds can grasp the plan of salvation, justification by faith, and the various creeds
of Christendom.

Religion.—The religion of the Fjort is from first to last a religion of fear of evil spirits. According to Mr. R. E. Dennett, who has lately given us in his "Seven Years Among the Fjort," the clearest idea of the character of the West African that has yet been afforded us, the negro is indifferent to the God of the white man, because, being a God of love and mercy, he is not afraid of Him. But of his own gods, who are all evil spirits, he lives in deadly fear, and does all he can to avert the consequences of their wrath. The belief in witchcraft is universal, and persons accused of being witches are burned to death—just as they used to be in this country only a few years ago! But nkissism, the religion of the native, sometimes has its use, for if a man "swears off" from any evil habit in the presence of his fetish idol, he feels that if he breaks his oath he will die, so he always sticks to his pledge. In this custom, Mr. Dennett sees a possible remedy for the habit of intemperance more powerful and far-reaching than any teaching any missionary can offer. It is a fact that drunken natives are often induced to become teetotalers by the observance of this strange custom.

Says Mr. Monteiro: "The negro has no idea of a creator or of a future existence, neither does he adore the sun nor any other object, idol or image. His whole belief is in evil spirits, and in charms

or "fetishes." These "fetishes" can be employed
for evil as well as to counteract the bad effects of
other malign "fetishes" or spirits. * * * In almost
every large town there is a "fetish house," under
the care of a fetish man. The spirit is supposed
to reside in this habitation, and is believed to watch
over the safety of the town. These "fetish men
are consulted in all cases of sickness or death, as
also to work charms in favor of, and against every
imaginable thing: for luck, health, rain, good crops,
fecundity; against all illness, storms, fire, surf and
misfortunes, and calamities of every kind."

Almost any outlandish thing may be used as a
fetish, from an elaborate wooden idol four feet
high, "its crown adorned (?) with old iron scraps
and bits of mirror glass" (Stanley), down to a
short bit of wood with a carved head, a pouch
stuffed full of guano, feathers and "tacula," and
even "a bundle of rags or shreds of cotton-cloth
of all kinds, black with filth and perspiration"
(Monteiro), suspended from the shoulder or hung
in a hut. A small iron bell, a large flat seed of
the *Entada Gigantea*, small antelope horns or land
shells, either empty or filled with various kinds of
filth, are all used as "fetish" charms, and worn suspended from the neck. Fetishes are hung in the
huts, also on the outside, over the door, or almost
anywhere. Some tribes carve in wood very

elaborate fetish idols, the finest being those made
on the Congo by the Mussurongos. In his "Angola," Mr. Monteiro figures one procured at Boma,
which is worthy of note. The figure is that of a
man sitting cross-legged, like Buddha, holding a
shillalah in his right hand and a ten-pin in his left,
while his hair has grown up over his head into a
huge mushroom, which covers him. The carving
has been remarkably well done, considering the
intellectual and social status of the sculptor.

It is impossible to describe here the manners,
customs, arts, habitations, and mode of life of the
Congo people. There is not space to even mention their huts of grass and wicker-work, their
weapons and utensils of iron and wood, or their
universal nakedness. Of their laziness, uncleanli-
ness, ignorance and love of liquor, I have already
spoken. Those who desire to know all about
these dusky millions will do well to read Stanley's
"Congo," Harper Brothers; Monteiro's "Angola
and the River Congo," Macmillan & Co.; Cameron's "Across Africa," Harper's; Mr. Tisdel's
Report, and Mr. Dennett's "Seven Years Among
the Fjort."

It is true that the people of the Congo basin are
unprepossessing and unpromising. It is true that
they are ignorant, indolent, degraded and vicious.
It is true that with very many of them, their habits,

and practices are revolting.   It is true that on the
Lower Congo and the Coast their "environment"
is not calculated to stimulate their development.
But when we turn our glance backward to the
barbarism which cradled the great Anglo-Saxon
race, to the savagery of the northern races which
shocked and appalled the civilization of ancient
Rome, and out of which we sprang, let no man
say that the future holds no enlightenment in store
for the African.   We have seen what a few short
centuries have done in Northern Europe with
what were once considered most barbarous bar-
barians, therefore let no man say that Africa is
not the cradle of a race that shall in time eclipse
ours.   It is dangerous to say what a race of people
will not do, or become.   It is idle and puerile to
say that the natives of Africa, or of anywhere, for
that matter, are not capable of improvement, or of
moral and material advancement.

In the light of the fact that the Africans are
more like grown up children without guardians
than competent men and women, is any one brutal
enough to say, "Let them look out for themselves"?
Can it be that any able-bodied, fully-equipped
man or woman is so destitute of all human feeling,
all philanthropy, all manhood, and all Godlikeness,
as to feel indifferent to the fate of the victims free
rum is making in Africa?   Are we so beset with

wars abroad, and internal strife at home; such
poverty, ruin and desolation around our own hearth-
stones that we cannot look abroad for a moment?
By no means. We are at peace with all the world,
prosperous and happy beyond a parallel among
all civilized nations, and rich in ways and means
for doing good all over the world. Our wealth
accumulates so fast we can scarcely keep account·
of it, and our credit is good in the markets of the
world for untold millions.

But above all do we pride ourselves upon our
moral and intellectual progress, and our principles
of universal philanthropy. Our native policy is
the policy of peace and good will. From the
pedestal of our goddess, we look down in sincere
compassion upon the less favored nations of the
earth and say to them, "Be as I am." In short,
there is nothing good or great under the sun that
we do not profess to be, or to do. And are these
professions a hollow pretense? If they are founded
on facts, then it is the duty of the United States
Government, "of the people, by the people and
for the people," to take upon itself the task of bringing about the total suppression of the rum traffic on
the Congo, if not in all Africa as well. Occupying
the position we do, it is our duty—it should be
considered a privilege—to take the initiative in this
great work to be done. It is our place to take

the first step, and it cannot be taken a day too soon. We can count to a certainty on the co-operation of England, Belgium, Italy, France and many other great nations. Let no cowardly craven, with a spirit that a dove would be ashamed of, seek to frighten the Congress of the United States or the people of this great and powerful nation, with silly talk about the danger of "entangling alliances abroad," or "foreign interference." If any such nonsense is ever allowed to stand between us and the people of Africa, then we are a nation of cowards, deserving to be publicly branded as such. No philanthropic movement of this kind need ever disturb, for one moment, our peaceful relations abroad. If this Government sets about the task in earnest, its ultimate accomplishment will be certain and complete. A Conference is the thing to do for the people of Africa what the Berlin Conference left undone—everything! If we dare not, or if we cannot do this work in Africa, that seems to devolve upon us alone for its inau-guration, then let us stop boasting about our great-ness, goodness and wealth; our educational, church, missionary and temperance work—let us stop boasting finally and forever, and acknowledge that our vaunted civilization is a hollow sham.

CPSIA information can be obtained at www.ICGtesting.com
Printed in the USA
BVOW03s1108251113

337264BV00016B/592/P